To our friends at
EM Industries
who inspired this book

A BETTER PLACE TO WORK

A New Sense of
Motivation Leading
to High Productivity

Adolf Haasen and Gordon F. Shea

AMA Management Briefing
AMA MEMBERSHIP PUBLICATIONS DIVISION
AMERICAN MANAGEMENT ASSOCIATION

For information on how to order additional copies of this publication, see page 98.

Library of Congress Cataloging-in-Publication Data

Haasen, Adolf.
    A better place to work : how a new understanding of motivation
leads to higher productivity / Adolf Haasen, Gordon F. Shea.
        p.   cm.
    Includes bibliographical references.
    ISBN 0-8144-2363-9
    1. Employee motivation—Case studies.   2. Labor productivity—Case
studies.   3. Organizational effectiveness—Case studies.   I. Shea,
Gordon F.   II. Title.
    HF5549.5.M63H33   1997
    658.3'14—dc21   97-7163
                                                                        CIP

This Management Briefing has been distributed to all members enrolled in the
American Management Association.

Printing number

10   9   8   7   6   5   4   3   2   1

Contents

Introduction

In our evolving global economy, we tend to look to capital and technology for competitive advantage. Effective organizations are also critical to global success. This realization has led us to various approaches for redesigning our operations. However, in the processes of "restructuring" and "downsizing"—tactics that provide our companies with leaner structures and flatter hierarchies—we often tend to overlook the fact that our people are the most important source of competitive advantage.

In many instances, the way we have made our operations more cost-effective has been to lay off workers—based on the simple notion that people equal costs. Unfortunately, we fail to realize that the success of cost cutting comes at the price of serious motivational problems for the remaining employees. The workforce is burdened with new responsibilities, and, at the same time, must cope with the uncertainty of further job cuts. Employee loyalty disappears and people's attitude becomes one of "to hell with this company." A recent AMA survey of companies that went through downsizing shows that employee morale declined in 86 percent of those companies. This leads to a long-term vulnerability for many of the restructured corporations.

In their mission statements, many corporations affirm that "people are our most important asset." Admittedly there are numerous examples of sincere efforts to promote participatory management and people involvement, encourage teamwork, and otherwise draw on the assets latent in human energy and talent. And more and more companies share ownership with their employees in the hope of gaining higher levels of productivity. However, we often do not comprehend that the task of turning employee involvement into competitive advantage requires profound changes in the role and philosophy of management, corporate values, organizational hierarchy, and labor relations. If these changes are not in place and, consequently, decisions are still handed down from the top, employee motivation suffers and productivity remains at low levels.

We need a different approach to unlock people's productivity. This may be an opportune time to revisit the principles of motivation, to see what *really* energizes people and lets them take ownership of their jobs. Since the 1950s and 1960s, when Abraham Maslow, Frederick Herzberg, and David McClelland developed their theories of motivation, we have made significant advances in our understanding of what energizes people in the workplace. For example, we now focus on the difference between "extrinsic" and "intrinsic" approaches and we understand how people's "self," their way of being, influences their motivational orientation.

This new understanding of motivation is the starting point for the powerful new concepts of *A Better Place to Work*, a workplace of high employee involvement and productivity. At the same time, we offer a fresh look at eight unique organizations, companies with unusual workplace structures that have given substance and credibility to the research on motivation.

It was a memorable and inspiring experience for both of us to travel around the country and speak to managers and frontline workers at these companies. The eight case studies included in this book were chosen to represent a diversity of businesses—some small (80 to 150 workers), others large (2,000 to 6,000 employees); some in metal fabrication or steel production, others in automotive manufacture or high-technology product areas.

In all our visits, we held roundtable discussions with people at different levels in the organization. Questions centered on job responsibilities and decision making, learning opportunities and workplace flexibility, the roles of frontline employees and managers, as well as teamwork and relations to co-workers.

The common thread of what we learned, and the logic behind these companies' success, is simple: The freedom of employees to act and to control their jobs, their reliance on a different kind of management, their competence and flexibility, and the stimulus of working in close-knit teams have definitely made a difference. The implications of this are also obvious: It is time to put the people back into the center of our companies' universe.

The chapters that follow weave case study information—company histories and reports on our interviews with workers and managers at the companies we visited—with discussions of the new, more substantial understanding of motivation that has emerged in recent years. The two threads work together: The discussions of motivational theory provide insight into the deeper reasons these companies have been successful, and the case studies provide opportunity for testing, refining, and applying the motivational theory.

1

Jamestown Advanced Products, Inc.: Where Workers Run the Shop

It's impossible to characterize Jamestown Advanced Products, Inc., the Jamestown, New York, manufacturer of fabricated metal products, without saying something about the company's president and founder, Jon Wehrenberg. Wehrenberg is a mixture of nonconformist rebel and self-made innovator. Unwilling, himself, to work under the command-and-control structure that typifies much of the industry, he has built an organization that grants employees an unusual degree of personal autonomy and decision-making power on the job.

Jamestown Advanced manufactures a wide variety of heavy-gauge steel products, ranging from plumbing items and recreational park grills to a virtually indestructible mailbox (to thwart teenage drive-by vandals). The plant occupies space in the Jamestown, New York, industrial park at the city airport and employs approximately eighty people.

Jamestown is a diversified industrial city of about thirty-five thousand people at the southern end of Lake Chautauqua, about

1

an hour's drive south of Buffalo, New York, and a similar distance east of Erie, Pennsylvania. The company's workforce is a blue-collar, skilled-trades group composed predominantly of welders and machine operators. Although its products are not high-tech, they are sophisticated; the work is subtle and requires considerable skill.

The Personal Perspective

In his early career, as a design-draftsman for American Sterilizer and later as the company's manager of product development, Jon Wehrenberg enjoyed the independence of his job as well as the satisfaction of bringing new ideas to market. Then one day in the late 1970s, everything changed. New management took over at American Sterilizer. Jon's freedom to produce and to make his own decisions ended. The new bosses reminded Wehrenberg that he lacked formal education, a shortcoming that would henceforth require closer supervision of his activities. From now on, decisions had to be submitted to upper management.

Gone was the fun and enjoyment of Wehrenberg's job, and his decision to leave the company did not take long to make. Some difficult years followed while he concentrated on being on his own. Eventually he found himself involved in turning around a series of bankrupt companies that had been run into the ground by inefficient management. He discovered that he enjoyed that kind of challenge.

The turnarounds provided a series of learning experiences on the importance of teamwork, the power of independent thought, and the inherent potential for creativity in people. He began to develop and apply his own ideas about management, based on these experiences. And he became more skilled and experienced in metal fabrication. He sold his last turnaround at a substantial profit.

Wehrenberg's success in metal fabrication led to the inception of Jamestown Advanced. A company that knew of his skills was looking for a reliable domestic supplier for a fabricated piece the company was then importing from Asia. Obviously prices had to be competitive with the foreign supplier.

Wehrenberg went to work on two fronts. Because labor was a major cost factor for the fabricated piece, he redesigned the component to reduce the labor content. At the same time, he hired an experienced crew of metal workers, explained the task and the challenge at hand, and struck a unique arrangement with them: He would provide a productivity bonus based on the difference between the estimated labor cost to produce the part and the actual labor costs. If workers could reduce the labor costs once production was in full swing, and do so without compromising quality, they would receive the cost savings.

Wehrenberg's agreement with the customer provided for a firm three-year contract as well as financing for state-of-the-art metalworking equipment needed to produce high-quality fabrication. The rest is history: The company's sales have tripled in seven years.

The Company Perspective

Jamestown Advanced Products, Inc., differs from most of the manufacturing firms in the local area in several significant ways.

1. Employees are in control. Workers not only have the power to run day-to-day operations but also the opportunity to participate in designing manufacturing processes for greater efficiency. Once the labor content of a product is determined, company leaders and workers cooperatively figure out the best ways to cut product costs.

Actually this form of participation has been a part of Jamestown Advanced's structure from the outset, as long-term employee and welder Chris Roll told us. "I was amazed at what can be done to improve an operation," he explained. "Making a specialty, heavy-duty plumbing product was one of our first items, and we tried different techniques and different arrangements of laying out the operation until we had a list of improvements a yard long. We would ask the engineer [who provides only technical support] how this or that would work. Sometimes he'd say, 'That won't work because . . .' and we'd learn from that. Other times he'd say, 'Yeah, that sounds like a great idea, let's try it.' "

"Gone was the old method I've encountered, in other places, of supervisors treating you as though you were stupid, or stealing your ideas and later passing them off as their own," added welder Sue Roll, one of the company's longest-term employees. "Here everything is out in the open, so everyone knows who came up with a specific idea."

We asked how it was possible for workers to make labor costs fit a predicted profit margin. Sue Roll responded with reference to an earlier project. "First we had to organize the group to come up with a plan. Then we had to add, subtract, and move people around until the process flowed good. When we could move the product faster, it eventually just happened."

Chris Roll added, "Then the customers started ordering more and more products from us—because of their high quality. We began requiring more and more people. At one point, we had three shifts of welders. Everyone would try different ideas. We would keep what worked and get rid of what didn't, and then try more ideas."

He went on to explain that the first few large units required about an hour and a half of welding labor. "Right now it takes half an hour to weld one," he said.

We asked if there were yet more opportunities to improve the process. Sue Roll responded with a very positive yes.

2. Jamestown offers a simple, direct productivity bonus. For each component, management first estimates the cost of labor (not including fringes) as a percentage of the selling price. Sometimes the production people are consulted in arriving at this estimate. Then, when the item is produced, the actual cost of labor is compared with the estimate. If the actual cost is less than the estimate, the difference between the two is paid quarterly as a bonus. If the actual cost is more (on a single product, for example), this amount is deducted from the bonus. Most bonuses fall between $1,500 and $3,000 per employee per quarter. However, the bonus is significantly reduced if a poor-quality product reaches the customer. This helps prevent high-volume production at the expense of quality.

3. Teams and teamwork solve day-to-day problems. Jon Wehrenberg's experiences had taught him the value of a workplace in which employees could take responsibility for more than their own job. As he developed this concept, it led to acceptance of work teams, cooperation, and trust of management. Workers in each product area began to operate as a cohesive group to maximize output and solve problems.

As Brenda Hebdon explained it, "If there is a problem [in the shop], we bring the whole line in and say, 'What's the problem?' instead of putting it on any one person. . . . The whole group gets involved to fix it."

"But don't some situations require an engineer's expertise?" we asked.

Sue Roll agreed that this was true, but explained, "First you get together with your group and you ask them if they think an idea would work or not. Then you get the engineers in on it. It's like everyone works together."

4. Leaders emerge as needed. There was a consensus among the interviewees that the shop does not have appointed leaders. "We don't have a designated leader for the group," Sue said. "Leaders and followers grow out of the group naturally. However, we do tend to follow those who have been here longer, that is, those who have more experience or perhaps better ideas. But basically we're all equal here."

"When a problem arises," said Brenda Hebdon, "sometimes we get more than one leader, and they may try to go off in different directions—they may lack cooperation. Usually though, we just do what needs to get done and don't make a big deal of it. But if there is disagreement, we get the whole group together and work it out. If there is a serious disagreement, we may take it to management, but that doesn't happen very often."

5. Management takes on a new role. There was general agreement among workers that they didn't need or want a supervisor—someone with the power to tell them what to do. There seemed to be a consensus that management was there to coordinate with customers, provide the shop with information, order materials, and pay the bills. Autonomy means something at Jamestown.

"A big difference between Jamestown and other places I've worked," said Dave Hartmann, "is here we don't have a lot of people watching us, second-guessing us, or blaming us when things go wrong. We make group decisions. Management decides what gets done, first, second, and so on, based on customer needs. Then we figure out how we are going to get those orders out. We lead ourselves."

The Results—High Morale and High Productivity

As the workers we met with discussed their individual and group achievements, their smiles were abundant and their enthusiasm palpable. The "self-directed" environment at Jamestown had clearly raised employees' morale.

The consequences for employee effort were clear also. "I work harder here than I have anywhere else I've worked, but I enjoy it more—and that makes it worthwhile," said Dave Hartmann.

"You have to enjoy your work," added Chris Roll. "Otherwise, you're just putting in time."

What Makes the Difference?

Jamestown has three unusually intense assets that contribute to both high morale and high productivity:

1. True worker autonomy—workers run their shop
2. Management confidence that employees can grow and develop as needed by the organization
3. A cooperative, caring environment and a willingness to stand by each other through good times and bad

This last point was demonstrated during a business slowdown in 1996. No one was laid off. Three people set themselves up in the office to do telephone marketing. Others were turned loose in the shop to improve operations so that the company could better handle the work when business took an upturn. In a short time, it did—largely as a result of the cooperative efforts of all personnel.

2

The Power of Motivation

As we ponder the developments at Jamestown Advanced Products, one remark, by welder Dave Hartmann, continues to reverberate: "I work harder here than I have anywhere else I've worked, but I enjoy it more."

What inspires people to work hard? What energizes them to perform at high levels of effort and productivity? What makes people strive persistently toward specific goals? What encourages them to apply their creative talents to solving work-related problems? These questions have created an interest in motivational theories as they apply to business and industry. And researchers working in the area have developed a following that includes executives as well as psychologists.

Some approaches have focused on management techniques and leadership styles that can generate highly energized behavior. Leadership is a matter of "Bringing Out the Best in People," suggests the title of a recent seminar. Harvard University's John P. Kotter considers motivational talent one of the important corporate leadership skills.

In general, however, industry still follows the motivational theories advanced in the 1950s: "Management by objectives," linking compensation and incentives to individuals' performance, and appeals to people's "need to achieve" all trace their heritage to David McClelland's needs theory. Motivation based on a "people orientation," along with a focus on company values like trust, respect, and loyalty, fulfill the "belonging" and "esteem" levels of Abraham Maslow's "hierarchy of needs." Motivational notions based on empowerment, supporting people's self-esteem, and practicing a cooperative management style can be traced to the ideas expressed in Frederick Herzberg's *Motivation to Work*, published in 1959.

Many times, however, these approaches are rendered short-lived and ineffective by their extrinsic nature and by the ways in which management tends to respond to people's needs by offering external inducements and rewards. As all of us have experienced, such rewards allow for manipulation and may raise questions about the honesty and truthfulness of the managerial provider. "Do as I say and not as I do" is still very much practiced in business.

In many circumstances, external rewards may actually be detrimental to people's motivation, as studies by Edward L. Deci and R. M. Ryan in the late 1970s have shown. When a worker interprets the reward as an outside "control," this perception may undermine the individual's efforts to preserve his or her sense of competence and self-determination. These findings certainly raise questions about many of industry's incentive and award programs.

Since the mid-1970s, new theories have emerged to focus on intrinsic motivational processes and on the "self-systems" that determine an individual's behavior. So far, management is mostly unaware of these new developments. Intrinsic motivation comes from the inside of a person. It is an emotional preference for a task that gives us pleasure and enjoyment.

The University of Chicago's Mihaly Csikszentmihalyi has coined the term *flow* to describe intrinsically motivated behavior. His studies show how flow arises from the challenge and the sense of control an activity provides. Moreover, studies by Albert Bandura, Carol Dweck, and Yaacov Trope on self-systems add support to Csikszentmihalyi's findings.

The latter research shows how our "self," our way of being, motivates us toward certain goals and behaviors, based on our view of our level of competence and our need for bolstering self-esteem. Some of us do not dare test the limits of our capabilities and are more interested in positive feedback based on current capabilities. Others constantly venture toward new horizons, expanding and enhancing our sense of self. Learning becomes a motivational experience, in particular for those of us whom Dweck describes as having a "mastery orientation." Here, the new theories seem to converge as we experience the excitement that comes from seeing our skills match a particular challenge in front of us. This, then, becomes a major source of intrinsic motivation.

Taken together, this research opens a new, broadened sense of motivation and encourages a fresh look at the motivational practices that we can use in our evolving economic environment.

A Better Place to Work proposes a new concept of motivation based on the following elements:

* **Job control**: Jamestown Advanced Products is an excellent example for our concept. People need full autonomy in their job, which leads to high involvement and total identification with the task. Corporate hierarchies as we know them today virtually disappear. The role of management becomes one of support and coordination: being available as a resource of expertise and experience, providing for open communications, trust, and mutual respect. Jon Wehrenberg's "cheerleading" role provides a good model for this new type of manager. People respect him for his expertise, and he is always available as a resource, supporting the plant's workers and helping them to coordinate their progress.
* **Learning**: People have their "self," their way of being, and their personal orientation. Learning opportunities are a

10

major source of motivation, as they allow individuals to grow and to acquire new skills in order to meet more difficult challenges. Our case study of The Apex Group, presented in a later chapter, will provide insights into the motivational role of learning in a modern workplace structure.

* **Teamwork**: Working in small teams, for most people, makes a job more enjoyable and stimulating. It allows for a work structure that gives the team responsibility for a meaningful segment of a task. Teams have leaders and followers. Therefore, people are able to choose the level of challenge they can accept, and can count on the support of and earn the recognition of their peers. In a broader sense, teamwork may develop into a culture of enormous motivational strength, as our case study on Southwest Airlines in the next chapter will show. Southwest employees are one big team, and the team has reached an astounding productivity level.

There seems to be no limit to what the productive energies of motivated workers are able to accomplish. As Opel, GM's German subsidiary, expresses it in a brochure describing the plant's new production system: "Employee motivation represents one of our largest productivity reserves and is therefore a key element for increasing the international competitiveness of German automobile manufacturers." Opel is right: In today's global economy, employee productivity is probably the most important success factor in a competitive business.

Professor Edward E. Lawler III of the University of Southern California, Los Angeles, makes an important point, based on his extensive studies on high worker involvement: To be effective, the principles of involvement and self-management require significant change in the structure of organizations, beginning with the role and philosophy of management.

The manager who seeks to build "a better place to work" will be a coordinator, a coach, and a mentor to his co-workers.

The manager's power will no longer come from the "legitimacy" of a position in the corporate hierarchy, but from being respected as a role model for the organization and for having superior expertise and experience.

Management and Motivation

All of the companies we visited provided solid evidence of how this new role for management can shape a dynamic workplace. Moreover, each company demonstrated a blending of the three galvanizing elements of motivation: autonomy, learning, and teamwork. At some companies, one element stood out as a driving force—autonomy at Jamestown Advanced, for example.

Before going further, let's complete the triad by looking at two more case studies. One demonstrates the preeminence of teamwork; the other puts learning at the center of the action.

3

Southwest Airlines: The Culture of "LUV"

In 1996, when Southwest Airlines marked its twenty-fifth anniversary, it had good reason to celebrate.

While its big competitors, American, Delta, and United, lost billions of dollars in the early 1990s, fifth-largest Southwest remained consistently profitable. For four consecutive years, the company won the unofficial "Triple Crown" of the airline industry—for fewest complaints, fewest delays, and fewest mishandled bags, based on statistics published by the U.S. Department of Transportation. Moreover, the Department of Transportation went on record as calling Southwest Airlines "the principal driving force for changes occurring in the airline industry."

Wall Street's financial analysts attribute Southwest's positive development to banal reasons like its short-haul no-frills service, quick gate turnaround, and low cost per passenger seat mile. There is some truth in all of this, as the comparisons of Southwest's performance with other airlines show in Table 3-1. Moreover, Southwest flies only Boeing 737 aircraft, which makes maintenance operations more efficient.

It seems to us, however, that the single most important factor for Southwest's success is the airline's "culture" in the broadest sense. "Luv," Southwest's ticker symbol, also symbolizes the

13

Table 3-1. How operations at Southwest compare with other airlines (1995).

	Southwest (SWA)	American[1] (AA)	Delta (DL)	United (UAL)
Revenue (in MM)	$2,760	$15,501	$12,194	$14,895
Net income (in MM)	$182	($81)	$194	$371
Cost per available seat mile (in cents)	7.0	8.4	8.8	8.9
Load factor	64.5%	66.3%	62.3%	70.5%
Employees at year end	19,993	89,400	59,700	82,160
Size of fleet at year end	224	635	543	558
Revenue passenger (MM)	44.8	98.0[2]	88.9	78.8
Average fare	$62	$136[2]	$127	$168
Employees per plane	89	140	110	147
Revenue passengers per employee	2,246	1,100[2]	1,489	959

Comments: SWA's low-cost status is clearly visible from the average fare amount, although the other airlines fly longer distances and international routes. The last two lines show the greater productivity at SWA. The SWA workforce turns planes around faster, which leads to fewer employees per plane, and handles more passengers. Both facts lead to higher profitability, in spite of lower fares.

1. AA statistics refer to airline group. Net income includes a $533 MM restructuring charge.
2. Estimates (AA does not publish the number of revenue passengers carried).

Source: Annual reports, 1995.

strong people bonds that unite the company. All of Southwest's twenty-two thousand employees are part of a large team, of one big family.

Southwest employees work very hard and support each other by assuming multiple responsibilities. You may see pilots picking up trash or flight attendants helping to load baggage. Turning around a plane at the gate within fifteen minutes may lead to a celebration, with ramp agents exchanging "high fives." "Imagine," says Kathy Pettit, Director of Customers and a ten-year Southwest employee, "they're celebrating the departure of an airplane!"

While Southwest has a traditional hierarchical structure, relations between management and line employees are very close. There is no "chain of command" and employees have the freedom to make their own decisions. Managers stay close to the operations by spending "days in the field," an important program for both managers and office people. Tolerance for mistakes is high and there is always respect and sincere appreciation for fellow workers. "People at Southwest are allowed to be human beings," adds Kathy.

Southwest's culture is such an important key to the company's growth and profitability that Colleen Barrett, Executive VP of Customers, created a "Culture Committee" back in 1991. The committee congregates about a hundred people, mostly line employees from all sectors of the company—a mix of Southwest veterans and rookies with certain leadership qualities. Their task is to preserve the spirit of Southwest's early days by giving recognition to strongholds of the company's culture and by promoting morale boosters like "Volunteers in Action" or "Heroes of the Heart." The Culture Committee may not be a strategic decision maker, but it certainly influences Southwest's business in subtle yet tangible ways.

The culture of "Luv"—as James Quick from the University of Texas at Arlington points out—provides "the connective tissue knitting together an organization's people so that they can succeed in the face of challenges and opportunities." Southwest employees have the freedom to reach out to their fellow workers, to their customers, and, at times, to their communities. They are clearly the force behind the company's success, empowered and in control, working as one big team.

Twenty-five Years of Maverick Spirit

Early on, Southwest had to fight for its right to exist. Although founded in 1967, the airline battled in the courts for four years against Braniff and Texas Air, whose attorneys argued that there was inadequate demand to support three carriers in Texas. Those were the times of regulated air travel. Once Southwest was permitted to begin operations in 1971, those same competitors initiated a price war that drove Southwest's prices for flights between Dallas and Houston down to $13. No question that surviving these early battles created close bonds between Southwest's managers and workers.

During the 1970s, Southwest Airlines grew steadily as it opened service to all major Texas cities. But explosive growth came with deregulation in 1978, when Southwest expanded service to neighboring states and, most importantly, to California. Today, the California routes account for 15 percent of the company's business.

Until recently, Southwest's strategy has not changed much. Based on high-frequency short hauls and low fares, it helps to create new markets by attracting customers who might otherwise have driven their cars. Consider, for example, that air traffic between Chicago and Louisville amounted to about eight thousand passengers per week before Southwest entered the Kentucky market in 1992. Since that time, it has increased to close to thirty thousand passengers per week.

As part of its marketing strategy, Southwest forges close ties with the communities it serves. As a visible sign, the company uses the state colors from Texas, Arizona, and California to paint the planes serving those respective markets. Other aircraft are painted to look like Shamu, the killer whale, to highlight the airline's relationship with Sea World of Texas, California, and Ohio.

The reputation for establishing community ties may, on occasion, lead a municipality to request a Southwest route. When

Midway Airlines collapsed in 1991, the city of Chicago looked for another airline to which it could assign substantial business to Midway Airport. Southwest saw an excellent opportunity to create a major base in the Midwest, and CEO Herb Kelleher made a personal commitment to the mayor of Chicago to provide about a hundred daily departures from Midway Airport by 1995, a commitment that has been kept to the extent possible.

At the end of 1994, United Airlines mounted a serious challenge to Southwest's business by launching its low-cost "Shuttle by United" as a direct clone of Southwest's operations. United had ambitious goals for the shuttle, betting that the service could account for 20 percent of its domestic operations. Southwest responded with additional flights, and Herb Kelleher toured the troops in California to rally support against the company's giant competitor.

In early 1996, United announced it would pull out of all routes that did not feed its San Francisco and Los Angeles hubs. The Shuttle's business had achieved a dismal 3 percent of United's total domestic operations. "It's one thing to imitate a winner—and quite another to beat him at his own game," commented the *Wall Street Journal* on February 20, 1996.

The people factor allowed Southwest to maintain and even expand its strong market position in California. Southwest's employees are able to reach out to their passengers and make them part of the Southwest family in ways not seen at other airlines. Flight attendants may invite passengers into a game of "who has the biggest hole in his sock" or "guess the weight of the gate agent." At Easter, the attendants (who are usually dressed casually anyway) may show up in full-length bunny costumes to hand out colored eggs.

Close to 90 percent of Southwest's workforce is unionized, but labor relations have always been excellent. As part of the job definition, union contracts always include the clause "those duties historically performed" to allow for the type of mutual support described above. As of January 1995, Southwest reached an innovative ten-year agreement with its pilot union, linking pilots' financial rewards to the company's economic success. Herb Kelleher called it "a bold statement by our pilots that they stand ready to lead Southwest into the next century." Union president Gary Kerans agreed, praising the pact as "a positive example of good-faith bargaining in which the pilots were able to . . . prepare for our future together."

So, after twenty-five years of operations, Southwest Airlines is poised to march on to ever greater successes. As of early 1996, Southwest flies to forty-nine airport locations in the United States with a fleet of 230 Boeing 737s. In 1995, it generated total revenues of $2.8 billion and profits of $182.6 million. And behind this effort is a family-team of twenty-two thousand with a message, "Herb and Colleen: Keep up the good leadership!"

"Hearts in Action"—Southwest's Unique Culture

People at Southwest reach out to fellow employees, recognizing special efforts and accomplishments. Top management sets the tone: "Herb and Colleen" cards (from Herb Kelleher and Colleen Barrett) arrive for birthdays and anniversaries, or to thank people for a job well done. Scott Zirbel, a flight attendant who joined Southwest a year ago from American, remarks: "At American, one day you might find a couple of customer letters in your in-box, stapled together, without knowing where they came from. Here, each letter is sent to you with a note from Herb and Colleen saying, 'Keep up the good job.' "

Parties and celebrations abound at Southwest's headquarters at Dallas's Love Field. The walls of the cafeteria and hallways are virtually covered with thousands of photographs and mementos, a vivid testimony of Southwest's family spirit.

With praise being so persistent, we wondered if it had lost its value to the average Southwest worker. Kathy Pettit provided a telling response: "I don't think any of us hugs our children, our loved ones, or our parents to reward them. I think we hug them to let them know how we feel, and it makes everyone feel better." And VP of People Libby Sartain added: "People just love it. At Southwest, it means sincere appreciation."

Family situations are always considered and respected at Southwest. The people we talked with let us know (with considerable pride) that about 650 married couples work at the airline. About two years ago, Janie Tabert, a customer service agent from Indiana, applied for a job at Southwest together with her fiance. Both were hired. "It's encouraged here," explained Janie. When her husband moved to Baltimore to play professional football, Janie applied for a transfer—a perfectly acceptable reason.

Southwest's policies on "shift trades" also allow employees to express consideration for each other. Depending on personal needs and convenience, people can swap jobs and shifts. Flight attendants, for example, may work 150 flights one month and not fly at all the next, obviously within the norms dictated by the FAA.

Charitable outreach and relief efforts rank high on Southwest's list of community service goals. The Hearts in Action program, for example, encourages employees to dedicate three hours to a volunteer effort of their choice in a given month. The only reward is a T-shirt provided by Southwest, but generally almost everybody participates.

Many employees make regular voluntary contributions to the Southwest Employees' Catastrophic Fund, established to help employees cope with extreme misfortune not sufficiently covered by Southwest's benefit plans. Being sensitive to the needs of others is an important element of Southwest's culture, and the willingness to help others is not limited to the Employees' Catastrophic Fund. The Oklahoma City bombing and the Midwest flood emergencies triggered many spontaneous responses on the part of Southwest employees.

A "University for People"

From early on, training and skill improvement played an important part in stimulating development of the Southwest culture.

Training programs, now under the auspices of the company's University for People, are seen as motivational experiences that add to people's flexibility. The university's training catalogue enables employees to choose courses with appropriate subject matter and level of difficulty. The programs continue to grow. For example, a course on customer care, previously taught for Southwest's flight attendants, is now offered to other groups that have customer contact. Currently, training amounts to an average of sixteen hours per year per employee, but plans call for expanding the programs to about forty hours.

A Self-Perpetuating Culture

The people of Southwest visibly enjoy the culture, and the word spreads. It's not surprising, then, that the company receives about 140,000 unsolicited job applications per year, many of them from friends or family members of current employees. Over the past few years, Southwest hired 3,000 to 4,000 people per year, which translates into an unusually large recruiting and interviewing effort. Management believes it is important to find the right people, individuals who will "fit" into Southwest's family culture. Many employees help in the recruiting effort. One such employee, Beverly Brown-Preiss, a Southwest flight attendant for almost twenty years, likes the added duties. She commented, "Southwest uses its workforce in areas other than their area of expertise, which is neat!"

Not surprisingly, attrition at Southwest is very low, at about 7 percent per year. As Vice President of People Libby Sartain explains: "Leaving Southwest is like getting a divorce." At times, people who left for "greener pastures" try to come back, even if it means accepting a lower salary or a less attractive position.

Southwest's "Patina of Spirituality"

At times, observers have likened Southwest to some sort of religious cult. In response, Kelleher affirmed that Southwest had always retained a "patina of spirituality." He continued: "I feel that you have to be with your employees through all their difficulties, that you have to be interested in them personally. They may be disappointed in their country. Even their family might not be working out the way they wish it would. But I want them to know that Southwest will always be there for them."

No wonder that people "luv" to belong to the Southwest family!

4

The Apex Group, Inc.
A Learning Organization

The Apex Group, Inc., headquartered in Columbia, Maryland, is one of those high-tech organizations that is creating our future as well as serving it. Ten years old, 180 people strong, and growing rapidly, Apex provides software engineering services and network and systems integration to companies in need of leading-edge, product-oriented development. With extensive experience in information technology, Apex also helps its customers bring new products or services to market more rapidly and cost effectively. The firm emphasizes architecture-driven solutions ranging from standalone applications to network distributed processing and client/server applications, network electronics, network infrastructures, data collection, distribution solutions, and mainframes.

The Apex Group operates in one of the most competitive fields on earth, a realm where the technology can evolve to a new level every six months. The group's ability to survive and prosper in this arena stems, in part, from two related factors. First, despite its small size, Apex continues to build and maintain strategic alliances with major players in the computer systems field, including Hewlett-Packard, Bell Laboratories, (formerly the R&D arm of AT&T), Microsoft, Bay Networks ESP,

Cisco Systems Integrator, Novell, Oracle, and Seagate. Second, the firm does an exemplary job of not only attracting but also retaining talented and flexible people and putting their talents to productive use.

The two factors are related, in that the firm's ability to provide high levels of service, respond quickly to customer needs, and keep abreast with technology depends on its employees. As Senior Vice President John Shetrone, Jr., told us, "When we say 'our people are our product,' we're not just spouting rhetoric. The secret of our success resides in the minds of our people, in their know-how, skills, insights, and ideas. The equipment we use is available to any company. This means that we have to depend on the *inner* or *intrinsic* motivation of people to give us the very best performance they are capable of achieving. Our job in management is to create an environment that allows the talents of our people to flow."

One might challenge Shetrone by pointing out that, like technology, *high-skilled people* are also available to any company. Competition for talent is intense. Signing bonuses hover in the $5,000 range, and employees shift allegiance with the ease of a resume posted on the Internet.

As we reflected on Shetrone's comment, and as we talked with employees in the company, we realized that he had put his finger on a fundamental reason for Apex's success. The company indeed has built an environment in which motivation is palpable. Moreover, we learned, Apex enjoys a turnover rate far lower than competitors. People tend to stay with the company, supporting its history of longstanding trusted relationships with clients.

Perhaps, then, the skill needed to hone a competitive edge begins with an understanding of what motivates computer professionals. Their's is a distinctive mind-set: They seek opportunities to be on the frontier of technology, build their skills, and solve new and important problems. Learning a new programming language, integrating technology to solve a complex engineering problem—these are the challenges that boost adrenaline. A company that does a superior job of tapping this innate motivation by offering learning opportunity will emerge with superior employees—and superior service.

But, like technology, learning opportunities are available to anyone in the industry. Perhaps no industry invests more in training. How Apex handles this area is distinctive and deserves special explanation.

Tapping the Motivational Reservoir

How does a company continue to mature its service offerings and technical mix while gaining competitive ground? At the Apex Group, the answer is embodied in the company's three-pronged Technology Advancement Program (TAP). The keys are:

* The role of "area" mentors;
* A comprehensive, guided development plan for each employee; and
* a system of testing or examination that allows employees to demonstrate competence in specific areas of performance for certification in each technical area.

We should note that the third area is especially important to employees as well as the company. Having a large number of employees certified in various technologies supports existing customer relations and provides the credibility needed to build new business.

TAP is a structured training curriculum set up somewhat like a college or university degree program. Employees have opportunity to earn a number of "badges" by completing courses in prescribed curricula. The badges are generally technology focused, but they can also be professionally oriented in a given field of study.

Many of the courses are developed at Apex, while others

(such as programs focused on management, communication, or other general skills) are available from outside sources. The company offers classes nearly every night of the week at the plant. Many of these are customized to meet company needs as well as help employees grow in their professional areas. It is not uncommon for Apex people to seek out the training needed to become certified in a given area of technology and then return to teach these courses at Apex. College courses can also be part of TAP, and some employees tie their development plans into earning both a college degree (undergraduate or graduate) and technical badges.

The company considers TAP as operating with a balance of company and individual investments—the company commits resources as an investment in its employees, and individuals commit time as an investment in themselves. With this in mind, let's take a closer look at the key elements of TAP highlighted above.

Area Mentors

The "Area Mentor" concept is a three-tier approach involving (1) *Mentors* who "own" a particular area of technology, (2) *associates* who are oriented toward absorbing what the mentor shares with them (so that they eventually become area mentors themselves—as the technology expands and diversifies), and (3) *students* who are collecting "badges" and completing courses across various disciplines.

The area mentor concept is closely tied to the company's approach to building strategic alliances, in that mentoring often focuses on developing personal competencies of high value to the clients served through the alliance. For example, in developing Microsoft Certified Engineers (MCSEs) or NSE's "OPEN-VIEW" capability, Apex set the goal of getting a large number of employees certified in such areas as messaging.

John Shetrone talked about the rationale behind the concept. "The mentor is the *champion* in [a given] technology," he told us. "That person needs to know more about that area and the relationship with the appropriate vendors than anyone on the planet. And that mentor's charter is to teach his or her associates everything possible about that technology, client, product, or service."

The goal, he went on to explain, is to push knowledge and skills down as far as possible in the organization. Anyone who shows the initiative and drive to learn a given technology can move up: students to associates, associates to mentors.

A Comprehensive, Guided Development Plan for Each Employee

To develop a TAP plan, an employee begins by seeking out intensive counseling from a technical mentor, supervisor, or manager in a particular area of expertise. The counselor explains career path options and training programs. The training can come from Apex, clients, other organizations, professional associations, technical schools, colleges and universities—in short, from any source that meets the person's needs.

Most TAP plans consist of an 18-month program organized in a series of bite-size chunks. The employee earns a badge at the completion of each chunk. Thus, participants experience many small victories along the way, gaining a sense of accomplishment as well as recognition of personal growth. TAP also allows employees with specialized backgrounds to explore alternatives for career change and broadening their perspective.

While the company will support TAP training, the employee must take primary responsibility to ensure that it happens. The employee is considered to be 51 percent responsible for completing the program, the company 49 percent responsible. This ratio is, of course, more symbolic than literal, but it sends a clear message: It says that while the company provides the resources, the person must take responsibility for the achievement of his or her plan.

Once the plan is in operation, the employee's mentor will

assist the employee in collecting badges, provide intense personal career counseling, and help the employee meet other developmental needs as they are identified. It has become commonplace for the company to send personnel to a vendors' facilities for special courses in the client's areas of expertise, pay employees' way to an association's special programs, or support a tuition reimbursement plan for work at a university.

Apex has discovered that intense counseling is necessary to make TAP work. As employee Kevin Nolan told us, "Many people want to participate, want to enrich their job, want to contribute to the organization, but they really don't know how or where to start. They may, for example, lack the basics in a certain technology. Also, when a person starts down a path and finds it's not right for them, they need assistance and counseling to discover a track that is right for them."

Moreover, the program has a great deal of flexibility, as Kevin Nolan explained to us. "What I love about these development plans," Nolan said, "is that we have a ton of badges we offer, some at a high level of difficulty, others at a low level. We can take anyone—a kid out of high school or college—and with some guidance, we can train or provide training for them to be anything they want to become. It may take them a year to get there if the goal is low, or four or five years if the goal is high."

We asked how TAP compared with competitors' programs. "I'd say you would be hard pressed to find some other company in this industry, large or small, that can match us," Nolan said. "Even if a person decides to leave the company (and few do) they have increased their marketability and employability."

Certification

The company also offers a variety of certification programs in the computer and related realms and assists each person in developing a personal set of certified competencies. This supports the employee's own development and professional advancement and also offers the company's clients assurance of employee competence.

A variety of means are available for achieving certification: company courses and tests, vendor programs, industry programs, Drake test completion, college courses, and college degree programs, as well as technical competence demonstrated on-the-job when serving clients.

Learning as a Motivational Tool

Our conversations with employees probed deeper into the question of motivation. Again, the importance of continuous learning emerged repeatedly.

As Kevin Nolan, self-described advocate, drum-beater, and cheerleader for continuous learning, put it, "I believe in the idea of the learning organization. I've read broadly in a variety of fields that affect this business and I share whatever I find widely within the organization. The organization that stops learning begins to die."

Paul Kenny expressed a similar view on continuous learning. "I work for the information distribution division (IDD) and manage engineering services. People get motivated every time someone raises the bar in our field, and our people realize that they have been prepared by their training to top it. There's no longer any job security today, but in a learning organization such as this one, there is a kind of security based on growing with the technology and staying ahead of the game."

Ann Marie Vignola, a network engineer, echoed this sentiment. "I don't think anyone in this company has ever said 'I've learned all that I can, or want to know.' We also learn a lot from each other even outside of work when we are relaxing or having fun."

Vignola's comment opened the way for a discussion of the array of ad hoc learning experiences that surround and supplement the TAP curricula. There is, for example, an informal "article of the week" practice in many work groups. One employee reads something interesting, brings in the article, and passes out copies for discussion. The article may relate to technology, to the computer business, or something much broader. In addition, some teams have their own reading programs. Team members recommend books and agree to discuss them. "We try to do all kinds of ad hoc things," one team leader told us. "We do anything we can imagine to develop our people with reading, learning, and observing."

One of the field engineers underscored the importance of the information that flows in from the operations side of the house. "People in the field learn things, experience things, develop shortcuts, network with other people (learn the tricks of the trade, if you will), then they come back and share with the rest of the company," he said.

While employees in other firms might consider meetings the bane of their existence, Apex employees see them as part of the ad hoc learning environment. They noted, especially, the learning that occurs in the engineering groups' weekly meetings, meeting with our operations people, meetings with vendors, meetings on product updates, etc.

Participation in the company's strategic planning activities is also part of the ad hoc learning, employees pointed out. "Our people present information on each year's goals and objectives and any system that has been established," one person said. "The experience we gain in making the presentations is valuable in itself."

We wondered if the array of learning opportunities might spark unhealthy competition, as employees vied for the most attractive jobs. Bob Blevens, a field engineer, set us straight. "At Apex there is very little professional jealousy or even competitiveness, because people are following the developmental paths they've chosen for themselves. Also, because of the adaptability that comes from what we learn, a person can float from one team to another—so you get a chance to work with and know just about everyone in time." He went on to point out that the company often invests tens of thousands of dollars in training and developing a single person, and that this investment doesn't go unnoticed. The company also offers a thousand dollars a year in college tuition on top of a competitive salary. "That also gets attention," Blevens said. "It's a powerful recruiting tool."

Sandy Woodward, Apex's manager of quality, noted that the company was seeking certification in the ISO 9000 and 9001 quality standards in preparation for its planned international expansion. Although Apex has done some work overseas, it hopes to develop a true global reach in the next decade. "Achieving the ISO certification will mean continuous training for all our people," Woodward said.

Finally, Kevin Nolan provided a broad perspective on what learning means for the company. "We've shown ourselves what a learning organization leads to. It's great for recruiting, for retention, and it increases profitability. It's also motivational to the degree that each person can develop his or her personal skill level."

Learning for Success

The challenges that engage Apex and similar firms are constantly evolving, with new issues emerging from unexpected sources. Constant learning is not only essential, but also motivating. Recall Paul Kenny's comment that seeing the bar raised is in itself motivating. When people believe that learning new skills will enable them to meet the challenge of a higher bar, they will likely look at the challenge as a reward in itself.

"We count on our people to be self-motivated—driven by intrinsic, internal forces rather than by managerial incentives and awards," Shetrone told us. "When a person achieves mastery in a skill or body of knowledge, they can operate independently and also contribute mightily to team success."

It appears that continuous learning and the motivation based on that learning is the essence of the Apex Group's success.

5

A Closer Look at Motivational Theory

Looking back at the first three case studies, we see intense people involvement and unusual productivity. The employees are motivated and enjoy what they do. They go about their tasks with a sense of purpose, and they take responsibility for the business. What, then, are some of the specific elements that foster work motivation and productivity?

At first glance, the three companies differ significantly in their focus. At Jamestown Advanced Products, the workers' motivation comes, in large part, from being in charge of the operation. They appreciate the opportunity to control their jobs. The smallness of the operation makes its cost structure transparent. And when the workers change the production process to achieve cost improvements, they see results—in both the company's financial success and their individual bonuses.

At Apex, a somewhat larger operation, the unique focus is on learning. In the intensely competitive high-tech field where technology can turn over every six months, Apex has developed a special three-phase system of employee development. Area mentors assist employees to write their personal development plans, teach their associates that will replace them, and support a client-focused employee certification system. People strive to grow and to increase their personal mastery, to be able to meet more difficult challenges. In a nutshell, learning has become a motivational experience at Apex.

Southwest Airlines, the largest of the three corporations, operates with a more traditional organizational and hierarchical structure. Nevertheless, employees are captivated by Southwest's close-knit family culture and strong people bonds that extend to include the ranks of management. Southwest's employees enjoy being part of groups that offer them the opportunity to be "human" and to settle into their personal roles. This allows them to earn the recognition and respect of their fellow workers. Clearly, motivation at Southwest Airlines is the outcome of a unique overall team structure.

While there are differences in focus, we see a similar impact on work motivation and productivity at all three companies. This may be a good opportunity to review some questions related to the theoretical aspects of motivation as a way of understanding why these companies are so dynamic.

What, exactly, has happened in the field of motivational psychology to make approaches based on the works of Abraham Maslow, Frederick Herzberg, and David McClelland appear to be ineffective? What is the "new" understanding of motivation based on? And why does it offer greater promise for building a highly productive workplace?

This chapter attempts to answer these questions by summarizing the basic concepts of motivation from both older and newer research. While some of the theoretical work cited here may appear to be far removed from the job of managing a company, it offers important clues for understanding why the organizations covered in our case studies have been so successful.

Motivation and Productivity

Although motivation can not be observed directly, it leads to observable behavior. This, in turn may have a desirable outcome such as high productivity. The word *motive* means "something that causes people to act." Early motivational psychologists tended to see the causes of action (motives) in terms of needs, or as Maslow put it, "Man is a wanting animal." Thus the psychologists assembled a list of needs that were thought to influence people's behavior. Research focused, specifically, on achievement, power, and affiliation—needs that were thought likely to have a behavioral impact in work settings.

This somewhat simplistic logic was changed in the 1950s. Psychologists realized that people may have prior experiences or expectations that prompt them to think about their choices in certain ways. A focus on how the human mind stored, processed, and analyzed information before acting gave rise to what is known as cognitive psychology. Other research looked at how a situation or environment, such as organizational structure and company culture, influenced people's behavior. This brought the impact of working conditions and other job-related factors into sharper focus.

In summary, attention to three determinants of behavior—motives, cognitive choice, and situation—provided the essence for a variety of theories of motivation that were advanced in the 1950s and continue to guide many of today's motivational approaches. The "effective" formulas of people management, the corporate hierarchies with skillfully devised titles and status-related insignia, and the quid pro quo of corporate incentive plans draw heavily on those earlier theories.

Today's view of motivational psychology points to a different concept. Motivation is no longer solely a function of people's needs or choices; rather, motivation itself is a "desirable outcome" based on the ability to control one's job (as in the case of Jamestown Advanced Products), on acquiring new skills (as in the case of Apex), and on being part of a team (as Southwest's "Luv" team demonstrates).

Viewed this way, motivation becomes almost synonymous with high performance. To clarify this concept, consider the role of motivation in such fields as professional sports and the arts.

The winners of New York's 1995 marathon, Tegla Loroupe and German Silva, are interesting examples. Both had won the 1994 marathon, running under favorable weather conditions: a 68 degree temperature and 78 percent humidity. These conditions were similar to those in their native countries (Kenya and Mexico, respectively), and this offered an easy explanation for their victories.

But what happened in 1995, when temperatures dived to 40 degrees with chilly winds at twenty-five miles per hour? Different day, same results. How can we explain this?

Both runners had compelling emotional reasons for their special effort. Both were running in memory of loved ones who had died recently, in Loroupe's case just two weeks before the race.

Or consider the ten- to twelve-hour days that a concert pianist spends at the keyboard before a performance, the lifetime dedication of a professional ballerina, or the compulsive drive of the artist who works all night on a canvas. Virtually all artistic efforts carry very little promise of financial reward.

There seems to be no limit to people's productive energies. As with Loroupe's and Silva's marathon achievements, or as in the artist's dedication to a mode of expression, we need to go far beyond need theories and other extrinsic approaches to understand the source of that energy.

What Makes Earlier Approaches to Motivation Ineffective?

The important motivational theories of the 1950s and '60s focused on human needs. These needs were seen as a motivational force, in that people would adopt particular behaviors in order to satisfy specific needs.

Based on this understanding, industry developed sophisticated programs to appeal to people's needs for achievement and power, for self-esteem, and for social contacts. Managers were trained in how to evaluate, handle, and "motivate" their subordinates. Indeed, "motivational talent"—knowing how to get others to work harder—became a desirable quality for upcoming managers. Looked at another way, motivation was turned into manipulation.

This approach to motivation was strongly influenced by the work of Maslow, Herzberg, and McClelland. Boxes 5-1 to 5-3 provide a more detailed account of their theories, along with citations on their most influential publications.

While Abraham Maslow's "Hierarchy of Needs" may not appear to be directly applicable to business settings, his ideas on people orientation, with their focus on human values and the need for meaning and purpose for one's work life, have not lost their impact. It may be worthwhile to point out here that all of the needs in Maslow's sequence have an external focus. Even self-actualization has a Faustian quality of an ever-present, external driving force toward human perfection. Maslow conceived it as a "need." As we see further on, this is different from the joy and satisfaction of intrinsic motivation as subsequent researchers defined it.

Later studies have given little supportive evidence for Maslow's prepotency concept—the idea that once a person satisfies all lower-level needs, the need for self-actualization follows. While his theory answered broad questions about human nature, its usefulness for explaining workplace behavior was somewhat limited.

Frederick Herzberg's research, which expanded Maslow's ideas on the meaning of work life, proved to be more practical in its concepts and universal applicability. Its shortcomings can be found in the difficulty of an objective evaluation of the research findings as well as in the somewhat arbitrary differentiation between "satisfiers" and "dissatisfiers" (the conditions of the work environment). Nevertheless, Herzberg's work had considerable influence and led to the concept of job enrichment, a major focus of subsequent research. Also in certain ways, the

Box 5-1

The "Hierarchy of Needs"
Abraham H. Maslow

Maslow's book, *Motivation and Personality* (New York: Harper & Row, 1954), and the concept of a "humanistic psychology" that he created must both be seen in their historic context. Maslow proposed a comprehensive life philosophy to counter Sigmund Freud's psychoanalysis as well as the behaviorist school of psychology, with its stimulus-and-response approach to motivating others. Maslow believed in the potential of humans to exercise choice, to grow, and to arrive at a point of self-actualization. Creativity, responsibility, and self-actualization were concepts of no consequence to either behaviorism or psychoanalysis. Maslow considered this a significant shortcoming.

The central piece of Maslow's theory is a pyramid of needs:

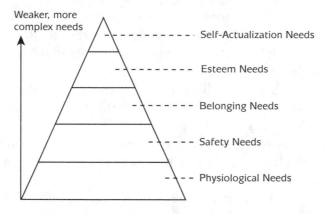

Maslow established the principle that needs generally must be fulfilled in sequence, starting from the physiological needs. According to his "prepotency principle," satisfying a lower-order need would enable a person to focus on the next higher need. Maslow's main focus, however, was on self-actualization. The drive for self-actualization might well advance even if there were a deficiency in a lower-order need.

Box 5-2

The "Two-Factor" Theory
Frederick Herzberg

Central to Herzberg's work is the so-called "two-factor theory," based on research of the job attitudes of two hundred middle managers, mostly engineers and accountants. The study identified "job satisfiers" (later called "motivators"), defined as positive experiences that heighten job motivation. In addition, Herzberg listed "job dissatisfiers" (or "hygiene factors"), which were environmental and situational conditions that might lower job motivation if not properly structured.

The research asked people to think back to an experience that made them feel very good about what happened and then, alternatively, to recall experiences that made them feel bad. Analysis of these experiences led to the two categories mentioned above. The hygiene factors (dissatisfaction elements) do not add to motivation even if removed.

The most important factors in each category were as follows:

Motivators	Hygiene Factors
Achievement	Working conditions
Recognition	Supervision
Work itself	Interpersonal relations
Responsibility	Pay
Advancement	Policies and administration

In its conclusion, the study recommended increasing both job content and job responsibility by letting people run and improve their operations. Herzberg also advocated allowing for personal growth and self-fulfillment.

For more information see Herzberg's *Motivation to Work* (New York: John Wiley, 1959).

Box 5-3

The Importance of Achievement, Power, and Affiliation
David C. McClelland

From early on, research in motivational psychology attempted to define motives or needs that would impact behavior. In the context of work settings, the needs for achievement, power, and affiliation were considered of particular interest.

McClelland's work in the area of achievement motivation brought two important results. First, he provided a new definition of achievement need, which he described as a "concern with a standard of excellence." Achievement-oriented individuals have a goal orientation: They want to do better than others, exceed their own past performance, or beat the goals set in the business plan. Secondly, McClelland's research group perfected a testing instrument, TAT (Thematic Apperception Test), based on the interpretation of certain pictorial materials.

TAT testing has proved to be reliable in measuring the achievement motive. This has greatly promoted its use in industry. An achievement-oriented individual is hard-working, intense, and persistent. He or she sets goals and expects success.

For more information, see McClelland's *The Achievement Motive* (New York: Appleton-Century Crofts, 1953).

---

current interest in the concept of empowerment follows in Herzberg's footsteps.

David McClelland's work on what he called "the achievement motive" was excellently researched and documented. A follow-up study, published in 1975, is interesting for its divergence from other findings. In this study, McClelland interviewed executives of successful companies in an effort to establish a pattern for a "leadership motive" based on needs. He was able to show that these individuals exhibited high achievement and power needs, but had only limited affiliation needs. This was somewhat surprising, in that interpersonal skills, being a team player, and many of the common social motives (such as love, friendship, and trust) characterize an affiliation-oriented individual. The executives interviewed for this study were not particularly imbued with these kinds of talents, nor were they driven by affiliation needs.

In summary, approaches based on need motivation have gained wide acceptance. Although this research has considerable merit, it doesn't get to the heart of the matter—the deeper emotional and mental phenomena that drive outstanding achievements in both our personal lives and our work lives.

A New Sense of Motivation: Today's Approaches and Theories

Much of our discussion has centered on the difference between extrinsic and intrinsic motivation. Extrinsic motivation arises when people feel driven by an outside factor, such as a promised reward. In contrast, intrinsic motivation arises from a strong emotional interest in an activity and a sense of freedom and autonomy related to it. Many studies have shown that extrinsic approaches work in opposition to intrinsic motivation by shifting the reasons for people's involvement to the outside.

For example, recent studies by Professor Teresa Amabile of Harvard University have shown that creativity will be highest when there is strong intrinsic motivation, while extrinsic approaches constrain and undermine people's innovative efforts. Evidence from these studies has significantly contributed to the understanding of intrinsic motivation. Amabile's work, among others, clarifies the importance of emotional preferences, the enjoyment of coping with challenges, and a personal sense of freedom and control.

Figure 5-1 lists sources of motivation and illustrates how our concepts of motivation have changed. The motivational fac-

Figure 5-1. Our changing concepts of motivation.

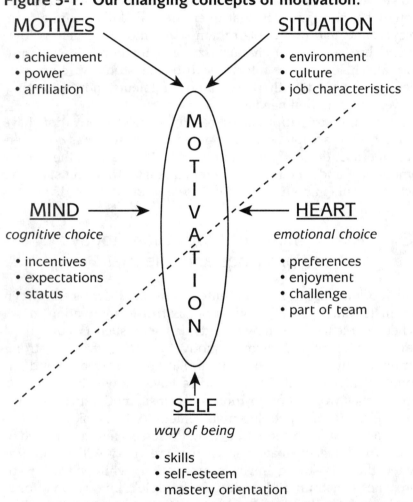

MOTIVES

- achievement
- power
- affiliation

SITUATION

- environment
- culture
- job characteristics

MIND →

cognitive choice

- incentives
- expectations
- status

← HEART

emotional choice

- preferences
- enjoyment
- challenge
- part of team

SELF

way of being

- skills
- self-esteem
- mastery orientation

tors above the diagonal line, which guided the earlier understanding of motivation, tend to be influenced by outside sources. Thus they lead to extrinsic motivation. The area of "job characteristics" represents a whole theory by itself, based on how job redesign strategies may improve workers' motivation and productivity.

The factors below the diagonal line illustrate the findings of more recent motivational research. These come from the inside, based either on emotional choice or on an individual's self-perception. Therefore, the resulting motivation is intrinsic.

It may be worthwhile to review some of the research on intrinsic motivation and self-systems. Box 5-4 highlights the work of Mihaly Csikszentmihalyi, whose concept of "flow" or "optimal experience" brings a new level of meaning to intrinsic motivation. Csikszentmihalyi's work provides the foundation for developing powerful new motivational approaches.

People experience flow when their involvement with a task is fun, when they enjoy a particular challenge, and when they feel a sense of control in being able to cope with that challenge. Learning new skills bolsters people's self-confidence and leads to personal growth. "Flow" experiences induce people to reengage in certain activities with even more energy. The result is a highly productive environment.

Several other areas of research complement Csikszentmihalyi's work, providing a more complete picture of what influences human endeavor. These concepts are summarized in Box 5-5.

Research on Teamwork as Motivation

In the area of teamwork and its potential for enhancing motivation, the work of Harvard University's Professor Richard Hackman deserves special note. Hackman's work suggests that the motivational structure of a group task strongly influences the group's productivity. By "motivational structure," we mean a team's ability to carry out a meaningful task, one requiring multiple skills, different roles for team members, and collective responsibility for the outcome. This, in itself, will motivate

Box 5-4

A New Understanding of Intrinsic Motivation
Mihaly Csikszentmihalyi

Csikszentmihalyi coined the term *flow*, or *optimal experience*, to describe a period of intrinsically motivated behavior. His studies, using large numbers of participants in a wide range of professions and activities, were based on a unique "experience sampling method." People carried beepers as they went about their daily activities. Several times a day, the researchers signaled their subjects and asked them to relate their experiences at the precise moment they were signaled.

From this mass of data, Csikszentmihalyi became interested in a particular kind of experience in which people's performance seemed to be effortless. They wanted to continue forever in their task and to learn additional skills to master more demanding challenges. The fun and enjoyment of an activity, the sense of control generated by being able to handle a particular challenge, and the growth of self from a specific accomplishment—all these were typical "flow" experiences.

Even before Csikszentmihalyi's research, most of which was conducted at the University of Chicago, other studies had shown that an individual's ability to control or self-direct an activity would lead to intrinsically motivated behavior. Moreover, people would engage in such activity as an end in itself. This prior research also clarified the distinction between intrinsic and extrinsic motivation. If the activity is done for a purpose other than an end in itself—in other words, for an external reason—the nature of motivation would be considered *extrinsic*.

To understand the difference, consider a personal hobby, such as gardening. If we do it simply because we enjoy being out in the garden, we are intrinsically motivated. However, if we cut the neighbor's lawn because he helped us with something and we need to return the favor, our motivation is extrinsic, even though no tangible reward is involved.

Csikszentmihalyi went on to study flow in work settings, mostly in smaller companies. Although there was ample opportunity for flow experiences in these settings, they seldom happened. Tasks often lacked challenge and variety; tough management control and overbearing structures and hierarchies interfered with people's motivation and did not allow for flow.

Csikszentmihalyi's ideas are presented in *Flow: The Psychology of Optimal Experience* (New York: Harper & Row, 1990).

Box 5-5

The Concept of Self-Systems
Albert Bandura, Carol S. Dweck, and Yaacov Trope

The development of "self" has long been recognized as a goal of human motivation. However, only recently has research focused on the fact that people are protective of their "way of being." Self-perception is now seen as a powerful factor in enhancing or limiting people's motivation.

Bandura's "social cognitive theory" created a valuable framework for understanding self-directed behaviors. His model defined different self-systems as follows:

* Self-monitoring: People use feedback from others and from the task they are working on to adjust their behavior.
* Self-evaluation: People compare actual performance with their self-perceptions of competence and adjust their behavior as a consequence of this self-evaluation. They may increase their effort or abandon the task, a response that Bandura calls "self-reaction."
* Self-efficacy: The most important of Bandura's concepts, self-efficacy describes people's belief that they can deal effectively with a particular situation. When people set goals at the top level of their perceived capability, performance motivation is increased to its highest possible level.

Dweck built on Bandura's research to show how people's self-concepts develop into factors that guide their behavior. For example, people who see themselves as having limited intellectual abilities will pursue "performance goals" to receive favorable feedback on their competence. On the other hand, people who see themselves as having greater abilities will pursue "learning goals," reflecting their need for self-enhancement. This creates what Dweck terms a "mastery orientation" and leads, ultimately, to high levels of performance motivation.

These distinct goals are based on how people perceive their own intellectual capacity. Dweck's research suggests that individuals who pursue performance goals perceive their intellectual capacity or "intelligence" as something over which they have no control. In the case of learning goals, the person sees intelligence as incremental and controllable.

In a similar way, Trope's research confirms the importance of feedback in self-regulatory behavior. People will be willing to accept negative feedback to the extent that it does not deplete resources of prior positive experiences. Generally, feedback is sought both for obtaining a realistic self-evaluation and for bolstering self-esteem. Trope's findings suggest that priority should be given to esteem needs in a situation that may deplete the individual's coping resources.

See A. Bandura, *Social Foundations of Thought and Action: A Social-Cognitive Theory* (New York: Prentice-Hall, 1986); C. S. Dweck and E. L. Leggett, "A Social-Cognitive Approach to Motivation and Personality," *Psychology Review* 95 (1988): 256-273; and Y. Trope, "Reconciling Competing Motives in Self-Evaluation: The Role of Self-Control in Feedback Seeking," *Journal of Personal and Social Psychology* 66 (1994): 646–657.

productive efforts. At the same time, being part of a successful group is equally stimulating for its members. "Good teams get better." Team success leads to integration and togetherness of work groups, which, again, is stimulating.

Translating Motivation into Productivity

When we look at this body of research as a whole, several important points stand out.

It seems that intrinsic motivation, based either on emotional preference or on people's self-perception, is a much more powerful and lasting determinant of behavior than extrinsic motivation. Being in control of and totally identified with an activity is intrinsically motivating. Having the right skills to meet an important challenge, being able to grow and to master new skills, and following one's goal of self-enhancement are all important drivers and sources of motivation. And the opportunity to work as part of a good team provides even further stimulation.

This clearer view of motivation reinforces what we learned during our visits: To generate real, unusual, and lasting productivity, the interest, dedication, and effort applied to our jobs has to be intrinsically motivated—it has to come from the inside.

With this in mind, we take a closer look at the three elements that seem to constitute "a better place to work."

Control and Autonomy

Motivation is at its highest level when people have full responsibility over an activity or task. This means that they must be able to make job-related decisions, to dictate the speed at which they are operating, to change procedures and make improvements, to innovate and be creative. In short, people who are in control tend to enjoy and fully identify with their jobs, which makes it a rewarding and productive experience.

To let this kind of motivation occur, the role of management, as we have traditionally known it, has to change. Managers have to renounce the authority of their "office," which is based on the power of the organization chart. The future manager must be a source of experience and expertise, earning trust and respect as a role model for the organization. His or her task should be to coordinate and inform, to develop strategies for the future (and to build consensus on how to implement that strategy), to be a coach and a mentor for co-workers. It's a difficult role; the manager must learn how to avoid interfering in the day-to-day activities in order to let people enjoy their freedom and autonomy.

We will focus in more detail on this new role of management in a later chapter.

Learning and Personal Mastery

In several ways, learning is a healthy motivational experience. First, the very process of learning is highly satisfying in itself. Each of us has had to cope with experiences in which our skills were barely sufficient to handle a particular problem. Yet we managed to stay on top—an exhilarating and deeply motivating event. Thus, personal growth translates into the ability to meet ever more difficult challenges by learning and acquiring new skills. With time, people choose their level of challenge and develop their personal orientation. Experiences tend to be most positive when skills and challenges are in balance.

Second, learning refreshes us mentally. It keeps us flexible and helps us to adjust to changes in our business and in the economic climate around us. Creating this "learning disposition" adds to our personal mastery and self-esteem.

Third, a positive learning experience helps us understand the broader context of our business and the interrelationship of its operations. We see our role in relation to our co-workers' roles. We care about their efforts and try to support them. This orientation clearly supports a company that is striving for continuous improvement.

A number of the companies we visited had introduced pay-for-skills structures and productivity bonuses. Admittedly this makes learning more attractive. While paying for skills is an extrinsic incentive, the source of the motivation—people's learning experiences—comes from inside.

In summary, while the underlying reason for learning may often be to increase people's competence or to foster career development, the experience itself generally is highly motivational and inspires greater personal and group productivity.

Work Teams

Team-based organizations offer many different advantages and have, therefore, become the focus of extensive research and new organizational theories. Although much can be said on this subject, we want to limit our comments to the motivational stimulation work teams provide.

First, the work team becomes a kind of "social anchor" to the individual. It is enjoyable to work with friends and receive their support and recognition. But it goes further: Group dynamics impact individual behavior and foster a certain role differentiation. The work team generally allows its members to choose their level of challenge: Some individuals become leaders, others followers. Or someone may be a leader at one time, a follower at another, depending on expertise, inclination, and situation. In this way, the team approach leads to many positive experiences that bolster self-esteem.

More important, however, this organizational structure makes it possible to assign responsibility for a meaningful process segment, even an entire work area, to a team. These broader and more important responsibilities create a different and more satisfactory experience for all team members. Cross-training and flexibility within the team make the work more diverse and enjoyable.

Taking its motivational energy from job control, learning opportunities and a team structure, our concept of "a better place to work" is the paradigm of a new type of lean, very productive organization, formed by highly motivated people, and largely devoid of managerial hierarchies based on titles and status.

Blending All the Elements

At this point, the obvious question will be: Do we know of any examples of work environments that mirror *all* the concepts proposed by *A Better Place to Work*? And if they exist, what measure of productivity and business growth do they bring forth?

In our travels, we came across three organizations—L-S Electro-Galvanizing Company (L-SE), Opel Eisenach, and North American Draeger—that introduced work structures with most of the elements proposed here.

The results are indeed astounding. Their work environments are enjoyable, full of challenge, and bursting with high productivity. At the same time, there is a new quality of work life to these organizations, to the extend that neighboring LTV operations call the L-S Electro-Galvanizing Company a "country club," albeit a country club with exceptional performance. The next three case studies give you the opportunity to see for yourself what the new concepts are able to accomplish.

6

L-S Electro-Galvanizing Company (L-SE): A Unique Achievement in Labor-Management Cooperation

L-S Electro-Galvanizing Company (L-SE) is a world class, state-of-the art facility that supplies 400,000 tons of high-quality, pure zinc plated steel annually to the automotive industry. L-SE is a joint venture between LTV Steel Corporation and Sumitomo Metals Industries, Ltd., of Japan, which provided the technology. The plant is located within the old Republic Steel complex in Cleveland, Ohio. Construction started in 1984 and the first production coil was produced in April 1986.

L-SE is an unusual experiment. Senior management of LTV Steel and the United Steelworkers Union got together on a new type of contract, based on multiskilled flexibility, in which workers would have control of the day-to-day operations of running the facility. The agreement opened the way for a pay-for-skills

Box 6-1

Dissolving the Traditional Boundaries

What would you expect from a manufacturing firm:

* That employs no frontline supervisors?
* Where union employees make *all* shop floor decisions?
* Where employees have no fixed jobs—a person may be a shipping clerk today, a process control operator tomorrow, and a maintenance worker next week?
* Where employees outnumber management on almost every company committee?
* That spends 12 percent of its labor dollar on employee training?
* Where management shares virtually all company information with employees, including facts on financial performance?
* That has collected some of the most prestigious quality awards in the nation?
* Where changes in manufacturing processes are made through discussion rather than by management edict?
* Where the labor agreement *requires* employee participation?
* Where there is no thick book of shop rules?
* Where employees decide who gets hired, promoted, and fired?
* Where former supervisors serve on teams and provide technical assistance to them?
* Where all employees are on a salary?
* Where the factory workers operate in teams and often socialize together outside of work?
* Where the facility is called a "green field operation," despite being built in the heart of an aging rust belt environment—the old Republic Steel Complex in Cleveland, Ohio?

The answer is high performance, high levels of enthusiasm, and excellent financial performance—the conditions that now prevail at L-S Electro-Galvanizing Company.

system, which management would support with a huge 12 percent of man-hours investment in training.

The marketplace results speak for themselves. L-SE is currently the most profitable division for financially strained LTV Steel.

Management Philosophy

Plant manager Cal Tinsley talked with us about the early stages of creating what became L-SE. At the time of the startup, he explained, L-SE was one of five U.S. plants competing to perfect a new technology for putting zinc on steel (galvanizing). The technology was available to competitors from both Germany and Japan as well as the United States and thus did not in itself provide any competitive edge.

Management needed to create a success story "in an industry that was sadly lacking such stories," as Tinsley put it. To do so, management's vision went beyond refining and debugging the technology. "The challenge for a new venture such as L-SE," Tinsley pointed out, "would be that of pleasing customers with the other ingredients of a successful business—quality and service—essential elements that depend on the performance of people on the production line." To meld these elements into the galvanizing process, it would be essential for management and the unionized workforce to work together.

The first step was surprising: LTV Steel's senior management approached the United Steelworkers Union to discuss possibilities of establishing what is sometimes called a "high-performance organization." Discussions centered on the need for a highly flexible workforce that could dissolve the traditional boundaries between operations and maintenance. The pay system would be based on the degree of skill workers acquired, and the workforce would be mostly self-directed, with management providing technical and coordinating resources.

Second, at that time the choice for general manager was

51

rather fortunate: Don Vernon—a tough, no-nonsense executive with a master's degree in electrical engineering—was to become the executive vice president. One prior experience in Vernon's career proved important. He had been involved in the startup of another LTV facility, the Hennepin plant in rural Illinois, where he was initially in charge of maintenance before he became plant manager. Many of the workers for this new steel mill (built, literally, as a "greenfield" plant) were hired from the surrounding farms. "Fifteen years later," Don told us, "we had turned well-meaning farmhands into confrontational steelworkers."

Something had gone terribly wrong with the handling of the people. It was quite a lesson for Don Vernon, and it set the stage for doing something different for L-SE's startup.

The initial labor agreement between LTV Steel and the United Steelworkers Union was not much more than a framework—but a framework that could be expanded by both local management and workers, based on the operational requirements of the new company. In practice, this was accomplished by forming a number of joint management-labor committees, each dealing with a different aspect of the new organization.

Tom Zidek, president of Local 9126 United Steelworkers of America, pointed out the wisdom as well as the frustration of this approach: "Allowing people to manage things has built trust, but it takes a long time to get trust—and it is a very fragile thing." Cal Tinsley agreed: "A significant problem is making sure that the old baggage [of traditional labor relations] does not come back."

Most of these committees still exist today and assume responsibility for running L-SE's day-to-day operations. Joint committees, typically made up of eight to ten nonmanagement people and two to four management members, deal with the issues of hiring, pay and progression, training, and benefits (such as gain sharing and profit sharing), as well as with safety, process control, and production scheduling. A social committee helps bridge the gap between work and family by bringing employees together away from work.

Much of L-SE's successful joint effort hinges on the Pay and Progression Committee, which has general responsibility for the wage section of the labor agreement. While the committee's recommendations need the review and approval of senior management, approval has never been withheld over the committee's history. This committee's hard work and long discussions are best reflected in the sophisticated "pay-for-skills schematic," shown in Figure 6-1.

For example, process technicians start out at a basic skill level, which gives them the base salary for a probationary period of six months. Learning the different skill blocks that represent the different work areas of the facility enables a new process technician to earn about one-third additional money. Then, through work experience and additional training, he or she will reach an intermediate skill level in either of two major fields: electronics and instrumentation, or process and maintenance.

In most cases, training and certification for these additional skills will be provided by more experienced fellow workers. Certification adds another one-third of base pay to the technician's salary.

With further schooling and training in one of the two fields, the process technician can reach the most advanced skill level. This time, he or she will have to pass written or interactive tests that will establish the required level of competency. This, again, will add another one-third of base pay, leading to a combined increase of 100 percent of the initial salary.

Today, some of L-SE's process technicians have reached the top of the pay scale. This has led to discussions about what incentives should be used to reward further training, as it may be in the company's general interest to keep skill levels current and to encourage technicians to continue learning.

Asked about his views on the pay-for-skills program, Tom Harris, process operator and union member, said: "Money turns me on, but there is also pride and a sense of mastery involved. To some extent, you feel more powerful—more able—the more

Figure 6-1. The L-SE pay-for-skills schematic.

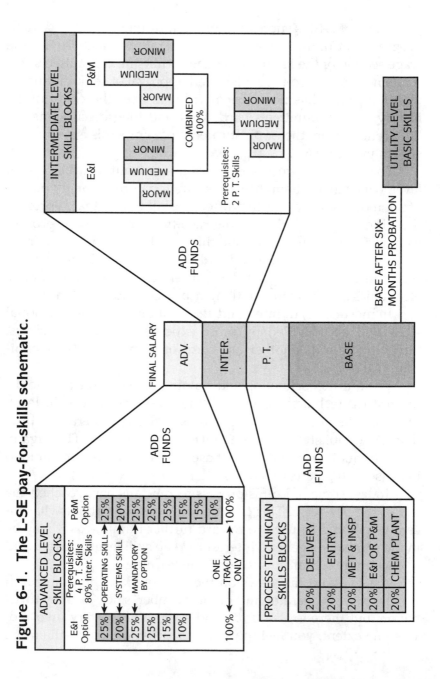

you learn. I would still like to learn even if there was no money involved."

The Gain Sharing Committee's accomplishments deserve special note. The difficult task here was to deal with the impact of substantial influences outside of the control of plan participants. The committee did not try to establish complex rules for any and all such events, but rather created a "fairness forum," which would review and act on the occurrence of such influences. While, again, senior management would review and approve the committee's proposals, both sides were able to create a climate of trust that would help resolve unforeseen difficulties. This committee administers a twice-a-year bonus program that awards bonuses of up to 25 percent of total pay.

A Unique Work Environment

The L-SE experiment offers a number of distinctive approaches to workplace organization. The following are worth highlighting.

1. Hourly pay is eliminated. L-SE workers receive a monthly salary based on skill level. There are no time clocks. "Control" over hours worked is based entirely on peer pressure and team respect. Seniority applies only to training preferences. Job assignments are rotated, either voluntarily or as mandated within each crew.

2. Flexibility yields cost savings. The multiskilled nature of the workforce, which allows for minimum staffing in the plant, has proved to be a major source of cost savings. Having five crews available makes it possible to schedule almost half of the "turns" (shifts) on weekends, when energy is cheaper. In addition, the flexibility of the technicians and the constant availability of trainees help to cover absences due to sickness or other reasons.

3. Diversity of work and control create a new way of working. The diversity of the work and the high levels of worker

55

responsibility make the jobs at L-SE different from work at other mills. Even an important decision, such as shutting down a production line, will be made by the crew, based on the factual situation and the problems at hand. In this context, former frontline supervisors have become an important resource in terms of their experience and skill level.

This way of working has proved very attractive to some of the employees. As Chris Vance, a process coordinator (who formerly would have been a frontline supervisor), said, "I enjoy trouble shooting and fixing things, so I still get to do some of the things I like. My job is to support the work team and help them carry out their jobs."

Neighboring LTV operations see L-SE as having somewhat of a "country club" atmosphere. Actually, however, L-SE workers will work harder and longer hours due to the multiskilled nature of their jobs. As Tom Schofield, a process operator, told us, "In one way it's harder to work here, because there aren't a lot of rules to follow. You have to make a lot of decisions, but you also get a lot of help from other team members."

4. Communication builds labor-management cooperation. Crew meetings are scheduled on a regular basis and provide for timely reviews of plant output and financial performance. Workers openly discuss trouble spots with management and resolve conflicts. Crew meetings are undoubtedly the major communications vehicle. In addition, committee participation (which both union and management encourage) provides a different, more focused view of the operation. A regular LTV Steel newsletter also plays an important communications role.

Don Vernon told us why communication is so important to the operation: "There is a tremendous amount of information to be shared in a place like this, and it has to get to a lot of people to be useful. The interaction also produces a lot of valuable ideas. I don't remember ever turning down an idea since I've been here. Any bad ideas are apparently killed in the committees, so I never hear about them."

Training and Learning Opportunities

To support its pay-for-skills approach, L-SE currently invests 10–12 percent of man-hours in training. This is an unusually high percentage, which may decline somewhat as more people reach advanced skill levels. However, as we suggested before, management may give consideration to continued learning experiences for the technicians and further advances in pay.

LTV Steel also supports learning outside the company. Company policies provide for tuition reimbursement, varying between 25 and 100 percent, for people to continue their education in related or unrelated areas. In addition, plans call for cross-training in the staff areas, using a system similar to that in production, to provide for more personal flexibility and new learning opportunities.

"L-SE is a high-performance, participative workplace," Vernon said. "We are considered by our customers to be the premiere supplier of electrogalvanized steel. The advantage of L-SE is not in the technology, but in the workforce. An environment of worker involvement and empowerment exists . . . better ways of performing the job and satisfying the customer are constantly being pursued."

The Big Picture

Since startup in April 1986, L-SE has continually improved in all of the areas measured, including productivity, quality, customer satisfaction, and cost to produce. This participative approach has provided a good means of achieving other successes, as well. L-SE has received the Ford Q-1 Award, the GM Mark of Excellence Award, and the Rochester Institute of Technology/USA Today Quality Cup in 1992. In July 1993, L-SE was highlighted in the Future of the American Workplace Conference, convened by President Clinton and Secretary of Labor Reich, as a successful example of a high-performance workplace. In April 1994, L-SE was named winner of *Metalproducing* magazine's Top Operation and Plant Award and, along with LTV's Cleveland Works, achieved full ISO 9002 certification in May 1994.

7

Opel Eisenach GMBH: Creating a High-Productivity Workplace

When Opel, General Motors' German subsidiary, set about to build a new automotive production facility in East Germany—the former German Democratic Republic—it did so amid increasingly adverse conditions for the entire German auto industry.

An article in the September 13, 1995, issue of the *New York Times* summarized the competitive situation. The growing strength of the German mark, the analysis noted, was threatening to price German cars out of the market, a condition exacerbated by inefficient production techniques and the high cost of supplies. The article went on to say: "On top of it all, the workers are among the most pampered of the world, working short hours, earning twice as much as most of their European counterparts and getting ten weeks of paid holiday every year. Small wonder, then, that the German auto industry is finally saying 'Enough.' "

German car makers have responded with a two-pronged strategy: opening new plants abroad and, at the same time, reengineering operations at home to make them more efficient. They are aggressively shopping for cheaper parts and pressing the labor unions for concessions to reduce costs and increase productivity. Average production per employee at Volkswagen's Wolfsburg facility, for example, is reported at 23.6 cars per year, compared with close to 60 cars per year at certain American and Japanese manufacturers. But, as the *New York Times* concludes:

> To be sure, Germany still has much going for it. Its work force is highly skilled and its economy remains the powerhouse of Europe. . . . And it boasts one auto plant that can claim to be a match for the Japanese: the factory Opel built in the former East German town of Eisenach after the fall of Communism. . . . Eisenach has been rated as the most efficient plant in Europe, with production of 59.3 cars a worker each year.

This short reference in the *New York Times* highlights one of the most exciting success stories in work motivation and workplace productivity in modern times.

The Opel Eisenach plant started as an experiment that would test powerful new concepts. It would provide full job control within a team structure, use learning and skill-based pay to reward maximum quality and to encourage worker flexibility, and promote a company culture based on open communications and mutual trust. As the *Times* article attests, the experiment proved highly successful: Opel Eisenach today is considered the best and most productive plant of all European automobile manufacturers.

From Automobilwerke Eisenach (AWE) to Opel Eisenach

Before the fall of the Berlin wall on November 9, 1989, AWE was one of two established car manufacturers in East Germany. The AWE factory produced almost three hundred midsize Wartburg cars per day, a model that dated to the mid-1960s and, except for a new engine, had undergone little change. Despite this, demand for the car far exceeded AWE's production. The waiting period for the Wartburg was seventeen years!

The plant operated with close to 10,000 workers—about six times more than in Western plants with comparable output. "The factory was filthy," commented Louis R. Hughes, Opel's chairman, who visited Eisenach in January 1990. "You couldn't begin to produce quality there." High absenteeism and poor work ethics added to the problems.

While VW, Opel's main competitor in the German market, focused on the other automotive facility in Zwickau, Opel aggressively pursued Eisenach. The goal was to become the market leader in East Germany. To accomplish this, Hughes put a two-step proposal to GM's management: Initially and almost immediately, Opel would make the final assembly of 10,000 Vectra cars in Eisenach. Second, with an investment of DM 1 billion, the plant would move into full production of Astra and Corsa models, achieving an annual output of 150,000 cars by 1994.

Opel's objectives for the new plant included aggressive use of lean production methods and labor relations patterns based on flexible teams and continuous improvement. As Hughes commented, "The East Germans have been so disappointed with their past that they are most eager to try anything new." In part, the anticipated work environment was based on GM's joint venture experiences with Japanese partners, in particular the NUMMI (Toyota) and CAMI (Suzuki) ventures. For this reason, Thomas W. LaSorda, who headed the Canadian Geo facility (CAMI), joined the Opel Eisenach management team. However, the envisaged production system in Eisenach went beyond those concepts, encouraging more worker responsibility and initiative.

In late 1990, the AWE-Opel joint venture completed the first step of Hughes's proposal. Chancellor Kohl visited Eisenach to drive the first Vectra from the Eisenach assembly line.

The accomplishment involved extensive education and training. To test and further develop the viability of its concepts as well as the abilities and skill levels of the former AWE workforce, Opel Eisenach dedicated a limited workforce of 240 people to Vectra assembly. Production engineers and workers had an opportunity to familiarize themselves with the continuous improvement process. A newly founded educational institution, Bildungswerk Eisenach, assumed the initial training.

At the same time, Opel began gaining market share against VW in the East German market. Both factors helped move the project into its second phase. Today, Opel Eisenach produces over seven hundred vehicles per day, with employment standing at almost two thousand people.

The Opel Production System

A 1993 public relations brochure on the Opel production system makes a surprising statement: "Employee motivation represents one of our largest productivity reserves and is therefore a key element for increasing the international competitiveness of German automobile manufacturers."

The observation is far from a public relations overstatement. At the heart of Opel's system is a revolutionary attempt to offset the world's highest labor cost by focusing on people's motivation. Our visits to the plant and conversations with workers during 1995 and early 1996 provide insight into this outstanding achievement.

In Eisenach, Opel moved away from traditional mass production techniques and put the people—their commitment and their personal initiative—into the forefront of the new production system. One premise was that working in small teams would foster people's involvement and personal contributions; another, that working on a larger sequence of the production line and having full responsibility over that sequence, including quality control, equipment maintenance, and ordering of supplies, would give people greater satisfaction and enjoyment on the job.

Within the new work environment, Opel relied on the front-line people to decide on details of the manufacturing process based on their experience with the job. Management's role changed to one of coach and advisor, assisting in moments of difficulty. Open communications and frank dialogue became key to this new environment.

From the outset, Opel gave its people the opportunity to examine all work procedures and restructure the work flow to make it more efficient, including improvements in materials, assembly methods, or equipment. Thus, tapping human ingenuity and listening to people's ideas and suggestions brought forth vast increases in productivity.

The results speak for themselves. Opel Eisenach became a record-breaking, highly productive operation and assumed the prime position among all European automotive facilities. Let's examine some of the unique features that contributed to this accomplishment.

The Opel Teams

Opel Eisenach operates with about two hundred production teams, each with six to eight members. Each team covers a particular sequence of the production line, called a manufacturing "cell," and owns full responsibility for the work to be handled within the cell. Because flexibility is one of the most important objectives of Opel's production system, team members are trained to handle each work station within the cell.

Acquiring new skills and becoming more flexible is important for people's performance evaluation. But flexibility has also a very personal aspect: "We can help each other if needed," says Hans-Ulrich Antoni, who formerly worked for AWE.

Once a team achieves a desired level of flexibility, the team may send one of its members to another unit—a temporary exchange that helps expand the concept of flexibility across the team structure. Alternatively, if no other program is scheduled, workers can use a fifty-four-minute overlap period between the late day shift and the night shift for cross-training purposes. The choice of where and how to learn is theirs. As Alexander Isinger, a Russian of German heritage who joined Opel Eisenach in 1993, commented, "I may say I go to the cockpit assembly and nobody will object."

The flexibility and the interchanges between teams also help everyone to understand the entire production system, as team leader Lutz Baumbach points out: "You get the picture of the interrelationships which may help you to solve certain problems."

Once workers demonstrate a specified degree of flexibility, they are paid at the upper, or *Facharbeiter* (skilled worker), level. Both factory workers and office staff are salaried, rather than paid an hourly rate.

Opel Eisenach's team concept may be the most important factor in creating work motivation and productivity. "Teamwork is a good thing and creates family ties," says Manfred Kaiser, a *Betriebsrat* (worker's council) member. "It integrates outsiders and ultimately leads to a harmonious work unit." "We get along well and after work we even go bowling together," adds Antoni.

There is a sense of belonging and of team pride. This originates, in part, from AWE's old "work brigades," which were "fellowships in distress" rather than teams in the Western sense. However, AWE's brigades bound workers together through mutual support, forming a prototype for the teams that operate in today's culture at Opel Eisenach.

This Is My Job!

Responsibility for the work performed in a manufacturing cell is clearly assigned to the respective team. It decides on when to rotate work stations, which may be after breaks, at midshift or from day to day. Materials are reordered "just in time" with canban cards that are picked up by messengers on bicycles throughout the facility. The cards are attached to material containers that hold parts for about two hours of work. New supplies are delivered on an hourly cycle by fork truck or hand carts.

Most important, however, teams are responsible for quality control and faultless workmanship. Practically all cars on the assembly line are based on customer orders and, therefore, come in a variety of models, colors, and options. The team has to make sure that each car is assembled using the right parts and that the assembly avoids any damage to the car body or paint. For that purpose, each workstation is equipped with distress signals (called *andon*, Japanese for "light") that workers may activate at any time by pulling a cord. This is done to request help (yellow), or to stop the line (red) if they see a quality problem.

At the time of our visit, Eberhard Kuemmel pulled the red light cord. His job was to reattach the car's back door, which remains separated on a support while the car body is painted. "Sometimes the support sticks to the car," explained Kuemmel. "If I forced it off it might damage the car's paint." A line stoppage under two minutes does not have to be documented nor does area or shift management have to be informed. It is reported only to a central control system so that recurring problems can trigger a problem-solving process.

The *andon* signal is the most visible proof of the extent of responsibility that has been put into the hands of the teams and their members. This high degree of job control ultimately leads to job satisfaction and stimulates productivity.

Who Needs Management?

While Opel Eisenach has a traditional management structure, the role of management has changed within the plant's production system. At the first level, team leaders are selected with the team's acquiescence. They coordinate the team's activities, schedule and set the agenda for weekly meetings, and provide advice and information for their team. In addition, they represent the team in other areas of the company.

The upper levels consist of area engineers who coordinate several teams, reporting to a shift manager. These managers have mainly an advisory role, based on their knowledge and experience. In other words, they stay close to the line in order to help in case of difficulties as well as to facilitate direct dialogue and open communications. "If there is no other solution, the area engineer will step into the line," comments Kaiser. And Harald Lieske, chairman of the worker's council, adds, "Workforce and management don't keep any distance in the manufacturing area."

That does not mean, however, that there is always full agreement between management and workers. Opel Eisenach has been in high gear for the last three years, which has put significant physical strain on the people. Future productivity gains will not be easy to accomplish. But management at Opel Eisenach tries to promote a climate of openness, credibility, and mutual trust, which is vital to maintain people's motivation and productivity.

Kaizen ("Change for the Better")

Continuous improvement at Opel Eisenach is part of the team concept. People on the job understand their immediate work environment and are expected to optimize the process, to change details of the assembly, or to develop new procedures. Opel Eisenach has established special *kaizen* workshops where people can experiment with new ideas. The initiative is all theirs!

As a result, the number of employee suggestions is quite high and has led to the German government awarding the company the number one ranking in their category. Standard operating procedures have been rewritten to eliminate unnecessary steps. "Our tact sequence (cell time for a production sequence) came down from 147 to 102 seconds," comments Antoni. Presently, employee suggestions average close to twenty per person per year and management pushes hard to keep that level. "With all the pressure once in a while a good suggestion comes up," adds Kuemmel.

Opel Eisenach's Culture

Special care has been taken to foster good relations between workforce and management in several ways. Principles of dialogue and open communications are key to the Opel environment. Bulletin boards and daily information sheets keep workers abreast of new developments. Office areas are open and accessible to everyone and the cafeteria is for joint use by workers and management. Maybe the most important outward sign of Opel's work philosophy is a common dress code of white shirts or blouses, gray sweaters, and gray slacks. The code applies to everyone.

There is a great effort to bring employees together outside of work. A "personal touch" program even provides funding for after-work activities among employees. Family days, hiking trips, children's parties, and sports events provide opportunities for informal get-togethers and foster a family atmosphere.

In summary, Opel Eisenach has been able to capture some of the community spirit of this town where the automotive tradition goes back over a hundred years.

Opel Eisenach's Lessons for "A Better Place to Work"

By far the most important message from Opel Eisenach's short history is that there is no limit to people's productivity. Opel Eisenach's secret of success is a team concept that provides an environment of integration and mutual support. Being part of a small family and working with friends is enjoyable. In a survey of Opel Eisenach employees taken about two years ago, 98 percent of the people felt positive about Opel's team concept.

There are two more lessons to consider. One is the surprising level of work motivation created by giving people full control over their jobs and letting them organize their workplace to reach the highest possible degree of overall efficiency. This changes the role of management to becoming a resource of advice and support, based on close partnership and open communications.

The other is the importance of learning, of continuous skill acquisition. Learning within the team and across the team structure at Opel Eisenach provides the people with a good understanding of the conceptual framework of the facility and everyone's role within it. Opel Eisenach is a perfect example of a "learning organization." Learning promotes worker flexibility and leads to improvements and innovation as well. It keeps people alert and adaptive to upcoming changes.

The outcome is unusual productivity. In early February of 1996, Opel Eisenach reported that it produced 160,000 vehicles in 1995, an incredible 20 percent increase over 1994.

8

North American Draeger: Changing the Traditional Workplace

Undoubtedly, one of the major objections to introducing the concepts of *A Better Place to Work* will be that it seems "impossible" to change an existing workplace structure. While we agree that our ideas of a better workplace are easier to install in "greenfield" situations, North American Draeger (NAD) provides an excellent example of how a company transformed a traditional organization into a highly productive and revitalized workplace structure.

North American Draeger, headquartered in Telford, Pennsylvania, is the market leader in anesthesia equipment. Demand for NAD products has always been high. In 1990, the company's 115 workers in manufacturing and quality control were putting in up to 25 percent overtime in their struggle to keep up with customer orders. Today, 75 people handle higher production levels, with overtime reduced to a meager 3 percent. While it took over fifty days to assemble one of their Narkomed machines in 1990, it now takes only ten days!

Don Trauger, now with NAD for eight years, summed it up by telling us what it was like to work for his prior employer, a company that subsequently went out of business: "For thirty years, I had my supervisor tell me day in and day out what I would do. I never knew [what I would be told to do] the next day. Now I know exactly what's going on and nobody tells me anything. It makes you really feel you are part of the company."

North American Draeger before 1990

NAD's manufacturing operations, directed by a long-standing manager who was well liked by the people and supported by top management, had expanded significantly over time. The plant used a traditional floor layout. Workers assembled Narkomed machines in different steps at segregated functional areas, each area stocking its own parts in nearby locations. Stockrooms in the plant claimed at least 14,000 square feet of space, not counting additional "overflow" warehouses. At the time, NAD had about 350 suppliers. Inventory was turned about 1.5 times a year.

When demand for Narkomed machines suddenly increased in the late 1980s, things quickly got out of hand. Parts were out of stock, production problems mounted, and workers stood idle. Unfinished machines were set aside and stood all over the place. "We had an emergency meeting every week," said Peter Schreiber, NAD's president.

It was not an easy decision for top management to let the VP of operations go and bring in Adri van Cadsand, a seasoned manager with a successful history of working with self-managed operations.

Knowing that their old boss had been pushed out, workers were understandably skeptical about the new man and his ideas. Van Cadsand faced the challenge of introducing changes and increasing production at the same time. It was not going to be easy, and he told senior management that the change process would take several years.

Times of Change at NAD

During the next eight to nine months, van Cadsand moved forward cautiously. A few managers were replaced by people who had some experience with the new systems, but otherwise the new boss took his time. "He tried to start this thing by consulting us and letting us know what was going on," commented Chris Papera, who joined NAD in 1989 after closing down his family restaurant. "The way it was explained, I felt part of it."

On Fridays, van Cadsand stopped production and called meetings to discuss the new work systems being planned. The changes would include the formation of production cells, new responsibilities for all workers, fewer suppliers (all of whom would deliver on a just-in-time basis), and in-process quality control. Yellow and red lights would be installed to facilitate communication of potential problems and work stoppages. A canban system would allow production cells to reorder materials automatically. Moreover, van Cadsand would welcome suggestions on how to change the assembly process. Everybody would have an opportunity to learn and be trained in the new systems.

It was important for van Cadsand to win over some of the frontline people and let them convince themselves that the new systems would benefit everybody. At the same time, he tried to improve the current system's throughput by taking care of the shortage list. He no longer allowed workers to set aside unfinished units, and he improved materials flow by introducing a U-shaped conveyor system and taking down the partitions between the formerly segregated areas.

At the end of nine months, the first manufacturing cell was in operation, using a team of about ten people who had worked in that particular area before. The team chose its own cell leaders on a rotating basis, and the supervisor of the area became a "coach." His responsibility was now to troubleshoot and to facilitate training for the team members. Responsibilities were phased in over the next weeks, although the installation of the canban system took time. "It was tough going at first," said Earl Trauger, a twenty-year NAD veteran who worked as part of the first team. "We were still out of parts and had to work around them."

But the ice was broken. After a couple of months, the next cell was formed, and other areas started requesting cells. Although job rotation and cross-training is important for efficient operations in cellular manufacturing, training in these areas was delayed for a year, to help workers get established in their initial jobs.

The installation of the yellow and red lights took the longest time, almost three years, because of a long debugging process. Obviously there was a learning curve for workers as well as management. "When they were first starting to be implemented, those lights were all on," remembered Earl Trauger with a laugh. People appreciated the enormous improvement in communications that came along with the light system.

Today's "New" NAD

Our visit to NAD in early 1996 and interviews with employees gave us the sense of a productive and highly energetic company. Employment in the assembly operation, including quality control, now stands at 75 people, and overtime is at an all-time low. Inventory has been reduced by two-thirds, which translates into four turns per year. Stockroom space is down to 9,000 square feet, and the overflow warehouses have been eliminated. The number of suppliers has dropped to about 250 vendors, some of them exclusive for certain parts. Just-in-time delivery is a reality, with supplies coming in on a daily or weekly basis. There is no safety net other than for imported materials.

But more impressive than the statistical indicators was the picture of the organization that emerged from the conversations with NAD's workers.

People's Responsibilities

"Quality has improved tremendously," commented Chris Papera. Indeed, product quality has become employees' most important responsibility. To help in this regard, the company has introduced tridimensional drawings to highlight difficult assembly points. (Subassemblies and the final product are built to prints.) But many of the new ideas for maintaining quality are generated in work cell meetings. Many of these ideas result in engineering change requests (ECNs), which occur every day and get immediate attention. Although employee suggestions do not follow any formalized procedure, management recognizes the most successful work cell with a luncheon on a quarterly basis.

As parts are reordered with canban cards, the inventory situation gets permanent attention. Working stock for each cell is stored on a nearby carousel with front and back work containers of similar size and content. This allows for easy control. Problems are communicated by pulling the yellow light cord.

Each cell takes responsibility for control of parts quality in close cooperation with vendors. "We talk with the vendor directly and resolve our problems," explains Bonnie Pross, who has been with NAD for eleven years. If a cell discovers it has a faulty component from a supplier (a red light event), the area's coach, along with representatives from engineering and quality control, form a team to investigate. This team must report back to the worker who pulled the red light, and he or she has to sign off on the solution to the problem.

Keeping track of the work cell's productivity is up to each team. There is absolutely no stigma associated with finishing the day's work early, as cell members can use the remainder of the time for cell meetings or to follow up with vendors. There is an implied job guaranty so people need not worry about time. (The facility has no time clock.) Everyone operates with the implicit understanding that throughput time will decrease with more experience and process improvements.

The Importance of Learning

As mentioned before, people started to rotate jobs within the work cell only after they were firmly established at their initial workstations. The plant later moved to a system in which the area coach certifies a worker who acquires additional skills. In a broader sense, this amounts to a pay-for-skills system, in that the performance evaluation process takes certification in different jobs into account in determining merit increases. "If you don't rotate and learn as much as you can, it hurts your pocketbook," says Bonnie Pross.

The next step—job rotation with other teams—has progressed slowly and currently depends on the needs of other work cells. Obviously that type of rotation puts a burden on the other members of a work cell, who must pick up the additional workload. However, workers definitely see this kind of rotation as a priority. "It gives you a better overall view of what is being done," affirms Chris Papera.

In general, the emphasis on learning is everywhere at NAD. Open communications are a powerful learning tool as information on orders and shipments is posted regularly. The involvement with vendors as well as contacts with research for the development of a next generation of products are learning experiences. There may also be specific courses. For example, everybody has gone through statistical material improvement procedures, affectionately known as SMIPs.

The Success of Work Teams

The team approach is an essential element of the workplace structure at NAD. A work team is able to handle a larger segment of production or even a complete subassembly, and this larger role makes work more interesting and satisfying.

Many times the success of a team will reflect well on its members. Says Bonnie Pross: "When you're working by yourself, you may be doing something one way and never realize that there is an easier way of doing it."

Working in a team may not always be easy. "You have to work together even though you have your difficulties," comments Earl Trauger. In the early phase of the change, NAD provided specific training in team building. Even today, NAD has a training facilitator who may attend cell meetings and iron out differences. But rotation provides for a better understanding of one another's work and "everybody gets a chance to be a cell leader," as several workers told us.

NAD's Lessons for "A Better Place to Work"

The NAD example provides a clear comparison between a traditional organization and a new, self-managed environment. People at NAD are upbeat and positive about the change, as Don Trauger's remark quoted in the chapter opening attests: "It makes you really feel you are part of the company." Or as Earl Trauger affirms, "It's 100 percent better. You have more control over your destiny."

Most important, it is the element of job control that has led to a substantial increase in productivity, reflected in the reduction of both people and overtime, in spite of increasing volume.

But certainly one should not underestimate the experience of learning. "The nicest thing about going to this type of concept is that you don't stagnate," says Chris Papera. "Before, you did the same things all the time, and it was boring like hell."

Finally, the work team approach provides for the flexibility in structuring NAD's workplace, making it highly efficient and at the same time attractive for NAD's workers.

9

Labor and Management in the New Workplace

At the heart of *A Better Place to Work* is a need for change, in both the structure of today's workplace and in the roles that both labor and management are to play in it.

The Future Role of Management

At present, workplace structures are changing, but for reasons other than suggested here. As part of their ongoing efforts of downsizing and restructuring, companies continue to flatten hierarchies and eliminate middle management positions. However, these changes often leave the top-down authority structure intact, which does not mesh with or support our new understanding of motivation and productivity.

More substantial changes are needed and management itself has to become the "changemaster," to use the term coined by Rosabeth Moss Kanter. In the past, management was an indispensable element of the company's organizational structure, with managers relying on their "legitimacy," the power given by their position in the corporate hierarchy.

If we are serious about transferring job control and decision

76

making to the frontline people, the role of management has to become one of coordination, of serving as a resource of superior skills and experience, and of coaching and mentoring. In the future, true leadership and respect for management must have their origin in the excellence of a manager's sense of vision and expertise, and in his or her image as a role model for the organization.

All of us have different skills and abilities that make us effective administrators, engineers, or accountants. We earn different wages and salaries based on our contributions to the business and on the situation of the job market. But that's where any special privileges should stop. To be a manager one must earn people's acceptance, respect, and recognition, in a climate of openness, fairness, and trust.

The absence of authoritarian structures can open the way for building a company culture that is particularly creative and energizing. Indeed, the change in our management philosophy is the most important first step in bringing about the degree of work motivation and productivity that we have seen in the case studies of L-SE, Opel, and North American Draeger. This new philosophy of management is also an important perspective for another evolving concept, the growing incidence of employee ownership in large and small corporations.

Employee Ownership: Does It Motivate?

There are currently more than ten thousand employee-owned companies in the United States. While companies have different reasons for establishing employee ownership, it often comes about as the result of tax considerations or as a consequence of financial difficulties, leading employees to buy out the company to save existing jobs. In most cases, however, expectations are that employee ownership will create a stronger bond between the company and its people, with a positive effect on motivation and productivity.

Unfortunately, this has frequently not been the case. Substantial research on the performance of employee stock ownership (ESOP) companies shows that employee ownership does not automatically lead to improvements in work motivation and productivity. The reasons for these findings are very simple: In most cases, employee ownership does not concurrently lead to changes in management structure and the decision-making process. It becomes a purely financial investment that does not necessarily improve work-related behaviors.

At the same time, employee ownership—particularly in large public corporations—is an abstract concept for the average worker, who may see very little connection between his or her work and the company's overall financial performance.

For employee ownership to have a significant impact on work motivation, management has to be philosophically committed to the change in orientation, yielding substantial influence to the new employee-owners. The case study on Web Industries in Chapter 11 shows some of the pitfalls and difficulties of this process.

Similarly, a November 1995 *Wall Street Journal* article on the merger negotiations between United Airlines and USAir illustrates this point quite well. It quotes Professor Joseph Blasi of Rutgers University, an authority on employee ownership. Noting that United Airlines is 55 percent owned by certain groups of its employees, Blasi stated, "It's absolutely out of the ordinary for such a large company as United to consult its employees so publicly, in such detail, for such a long time and so decisively." As result of the employee-owners' involvement, United decided not to continue its negotiations with USAir.

Again, employee ownership needs to go hand in hand with a change in management philosophy. In other words, it has to be supported by workplace structures along the lines of the concepts of *A Better Place to Work*. With those in place, employee ownership will strengthen and reinforce people's work motivation and productivity.

The next two case studies illustrate these concepts. Our visit to W. L. Gore & Associates provided a dramatic example of how employee ownership, with natural leadership replacing authoritarian management, can produce high levels of energy and innovation. Our trip to Web Industries provided insight into what needs to be accomplished during the transition phase in which management yields authority to the new employee-owners.

10

W. L. Gore & Associates: A Company of Leaders

W. L. Gore & Associates's annual survey of all employees ("associates," as they are called) asks an interesting question: "Do you consider yourself a leader?" Surprisingly, year after year, over 50 percent of the associates feel that in some way they do lead others in the corporation.

The absence of a formal hierarchy makes Gore a unique model for a new role for management. Explains John Mongan, a manufacturing leader at Gore and a fourteen-year veteran with the company, "I don't believe that Gore is a hierarchical company, [but] I do believe that Gore has structure. Structure is necessary. I think everybody looks for structure, in their life and their work. . . . What we don't have is written structure that comes along with . . . appointments. We have a fluid structure that flows with business needs."

The Gore company and its people represent the very ideals of a new workplace based on leadership determined by followership, on fairness toward each other, on freedom to take risks, on self-generated commitments, and on consultation with colleagues. The company has been successful for almost forty years.

A Short History

"Making money and having fun doing so"—the business objective stated by the late W. L. (Bill) Gore—has been widely quoted, and the story of W. L. Gore & Associates' phenomenal success has been told many times in the business press. We will, therefore, limit our account of Gore's history to the company's highlights. Our main focus will be the issue of leadership and decision making at Gore.

W. L. Gore & Associates was founded in 1958 when Bill Gore left Dupont, after seventeen years as an R&D chemist, to pursue electronic applications of PTFE, commonly known as Teflon. The first successful product idea—a method of insulating electronic wires with PTFE—was patented by son Bob Gore, who originated the idea. In the late 1960s, another discovery led to the development of GORE-TEX®, expanded PTFE. This brought about a family of new products and diversified Gore's business into many different markets. Today W. L. Gore & Associates employs over six thousand people at almost fifty locations around the world. Its business success stems from innovative research and proprietary technologies with a broad spectrum of applications.

Gore is a privately held company, majority owned by its associates as they join the Associate Stock-Ownership Plan (ASOP). While Gore does not publish financial information, its sales have grown to approximately $1 billion, which would make it comparable to a *Fortune* 500 company.

More surprising, however, is the degree to which W. L. Gore & Associates' unique corporate structure and culture has contributed to its financial success. Bill Gore was not only a successful businessman and entrepreneur, but also a philosopher who put forth his original ideas about how to structure an organization. In a summary of the underlying basics of the "Objective of the Enterprise," Bill Gore talked about the enjoyment of working as an integral part of a successful team:

Fun includes the pleasure of working with friends on teams, the enjoyment of parties and celebrations, but also the knowledge and conviction that what we are doing is important and of high value to people throughout the world.

Bill Gore felt that authoritarian organizations went counter to the principle of individual freedom and stifled creativity. As a result, he developed the concept of what he called a "lattice organization," based on the following principles:

* Natural leadership, defined by followership
* Direct person-to-person communications
* Objectives based on consensus as to people's commitments
* Tasks and functions organized by individual initiative around responsibilities known and supported by a team
* Basic principles of:
  * fairness with each other and all business partners
  * freedom to innovate, take risks, and make mistakes
  * commitments to be set and kept by each associate
  * "waterline," which represents the concept that some decisions are more critical than others
  * the availability of "sponsors," who follow and evaluate the activities and contributions of fellow associates

The concept of "waterline" deserves special note. The idea is that any decision "below the waterline" (i.e., capable of putting the company at risk by affecting the reputation, financial security, or the future of the enterprise) will require special consultation. We will provide examples of how this works later in the chapter.

In order to make direct communications easier, Gore plants have been built in clusters, each plant limited to about two hundred associates. There are no titles at Gore—everybody is an "associate." With the exception of Gore's board of directors, there are no standing executive committees guiding Gore's operations. Although many short- and long-term goals form a mosaic of objectives for the company, Gore does not have formalized strategic or financial plans. Business objectives are redefined quickly and inevitably as market changes impact Gore's business.

As a result of the ASOP, associates have regular updates on Gore's performance and financial situation. There is an annual shareholders' meeting, and the company distributes an annual report to all shareholders.

Bill Gore passed away in 1986, but his legacy is very much alive, making W. L. Gore & Associates a unique example of new workplace structures. "The complexity of enterprise in the scientific-industrial environment of today makes the task of maximizing human freedom and potential a challenging one," Bill Gore once said. No question that he succeeded.

Leadership and Decision Making at Gore

In our discussions with Gore associates, we repeatedly asked how leaders are chosen. John Mongan provided one of the most insightful responses. "The flip answer is *followers*," he said, then followed by asking a rhetorical question: "Now, what is it that makes people choose to follow you?" His answer: "In some cases, creativity. In others, absolute trustworthiness. . . . I think an ability to make clear that you don't put your individual needs or your own self above the team's. . . . Track record has a lot to do with it. . . . When people choose to follow you as a leader, they have to have the feeling that that's a good place to invest their careers."

Gore may have a plant leader within a plant as well as a manufacturing leader. In addition, there may be several leaders of manufacturing and maintenance cells. However, there is no reporting relationship among those leaders. They all exist in their own right and communicate and cooperate with their peer leaders to reach consensus on decisions of common interest.

Leaders at Gore evolve in different ways: They may be champions of a new business area, product idea, or any other new concept. They may have a particular expertise that becomes important to their peer associates. Or they may just be senior people with good business judgment drawing fellow associates to seek their advice and help. "It is the existence of followers that gives evidence to leadership," Bill Gore once explained.

"By leading I'm involved with profit, loss, staffing, capital equipment, personnel, and things that go into running a business," says Paul Phillips, a group leader in electronics production who has sixteen years with Gore. "As a leader, you are looking to get something accomplished. And you are looking for a group that will follow you to get that task accomplished."

These examples give us some understanding how leadership develops and functions at Gore. However, we would like to mention two additional structural elements that contribute to the smooth efficiency of the Gore organization.

First, a team structure extends across the entire Gore enterprise. Recall that the Gore plants (which include sales, marketing, and administration) are limited to about two hundred people to assure good communications. Within each plant, working groups or "cells" convene five to thirty associates under a leader. These cells make the day-to-day operating decisions.

Second, everybody at Gore has a "sponsor" who follows the associate's progress in the company and acts as that person's mentor. It's an excellent idea, in particular for new hires who need orientation and help. The sponsor follows the associate's development and monitors his or her initiatives and accomplishments. In general, the relationship between sponsor and associate is close, with contacts once or several times a week. In addition, the sponsor has the important responsibility of serving as the associate's advocate in front of the respective compensation committee.

How are decisions made at Gore? We mentioned already

that day-to-day decisions are made by the cells. Must the group leader be informed when problems arise? Not necessarily, as John Mongan explains: "If there is something I can do, if we need resources or some help from another facility . . . then I would hear about it." In all other cases, the cell members would simply handle the situation.

There is a difference when it comes to "waterline" issues. Remember that waterline decisions are those that require broader consultation and consensus because of their impact on other groups and on the Gore company. "We talk about getting the correct group of people together to discuss that issue," comments Paul Phillips. Capital investment decisions belong to this category. Hiring is mostly a waterline issue, and Gore's many compensation committees are involved to ensure fairness from an internal viewpoint.

Senior leaders at Gore play an important role in all waterline decisions. A senior leader commands respect within the Gore community and his or her advice is often sought. Explains John Mongan, talking about role models for the organization: "[Role models are] people who have broader influence within the company, who have longer track records, more credibility, are involved in broader kinds of responsibility."

Arleen Higgins, a fifteen-year veteran with the company who serves as part of the HR team, gives still a different perspective: "You know everyone's waterline is going to be a little bit different. You have to build credibility and you have to build relationships. And as you build those, your waterline will sink down a little bit further. As you accomplish something or you take the risk and you do well, that waterline can drop a little more."

Higgins provided an example of the type of action that people in her position can take. About a year ago, when Gore launched a number of startup businesses at its Newark cluster, the company found itself working with local agencies to bring in temporary help. Higgins didn't like the fact that those "temps" were a different class of associates. It was "counter to the Gore culture." Arleen helped to develop the concept of a "flex force," flexible full-time associates who would work in different plants to staff startup businesses. While still in its pilot stage, "flex force" is already up to forty-seven people.

In summary, it seems that the decision-making process works well in spite of the absence of a formal hierarchy. Many decisions are made quickly by the people close to the problems. Others rely on the network and resources of Gore's senior leadership. Sometimes the decision-making process gets to be rather tedious but, as John Mongan says, "On the other hand, it's frustrating to have decisions made that affect you, that you haven't participated in."

Motivational Leadership

W. L. Gore & Associates is a good example of a different way to manage—the kind of leadership that allows freedom to act, personal involvement, and job control. There is no question that the Gore environment is highly motivating and productive—the company's success is vivid testimony to that.

At Gore, leadership is exercised, not formalized. And as new ideas are brought forward, they find followers.

11

Web Industries: A Commitment to Ownership

In July 1993, Robert Zicaro, a machine operator at Web Converting of Framingham, Massachusetts, had the opportunity to address President Clinton at the Conference on the Future of the American Workplace in Chicago. "I have ownership," he told the president. "Ownership must be real, not just the sense of it." With ownership, Zicaro felt the divisions between labor and management would disappear and exciting workplace changes might become a reality. "If you own it together, you are in it together," he explained. "[Otherwise] why would workers want more responsibility? . . . If you are an owner you have the responsibility," continued Zicaro.

Web's VP of Manufacturing Charles Edmunson sees employee ownership as a catalyst for more worker involvement. "Meaningful financial ownership in the company they work for can give employees a reason to participate," says Edmunson. In his view, employee owners *can* make a difference, because they share responsibility for their company and they are valued as people.

Creating an Ownership Culture at Web Industries

Web Industries provides slitting, sheeting, and flexographic printing services to other manufacturers in a wide variety of industries. Founded in 1969, it is today the largest custom converter in the United States. Web Industries has about 230 employees in different facilities throughout the country.

In 1985, Robert Fulton, the founder and owner of Web Industries, instituted an employee stock-ownership plan (ESOP) and started Web's transformation into an employee-owned company. As of today, close to 40 percent of Web's stock is owned by the employees. By sharing in Web's profits, employees are able to buy additional shares for the ESOP.

Toward the end of the 1980s, however, Fulton and his management team realized that simply owning company stock would not lead to meaningful employee involvement. Since then, Fulton encouraged people at Web to experiment with different structures of employee participation. At the end of 1991, Fulton stepped down and Donald Romine succeeded him as president and CEO. From the start, Romine initiated further changes to transform the culture of the company: He introduced the concept of self-managed teams, developed a vision statement with active participation of the workers, and set up training programs to help all employees share management responsibilities.

While Web's organizational structure has been flattened considerably, the company has maintained traditional hierarchical structures. As Edmunson sees it, this continues to be one of the barriers that must be overcome. "Both managers and employees are used to working in a hierarchical context, as indeed their parents did before them. They bring these lifelong cultural assumptions into the new workplace. And even though they may intellectually endorse the new system, their instincts are not those of participative ownership," says Edmunson. He sees further barriers in the lack of interpersonal and team skills and in the slow development of successful and effective leadership.

The Need to Learn

The example of Web Industries is interesting because it shows some of the difficulties in transforming an existing company culture. Both managers and workers have to learn how to deal with the changes. Managers need to become advisors and coaches. They have to accomplish the financial and operational goals by working with their people, by listening and encouraging. The workers, in turn, need new skills in leadership, problem solving, team work, and interpersonal relations. In this context, Web has instituted the practice of letting the employees visit customers and other plants to see other environments and cultures and to learn from these experiences.

Web's concept of "Growth through Ownership" (see Figure 11-1) outlines different "cultures" that have since become the focus of employee orientation and training. The introduction of total quality systems (TQS), for example, provided four hours of valuable training per month for everyone and helped to bring the organization together. Web plans to continue a similar training schedule for the future, focusing on other cultures mentioned in the chart.

One educational program involves "reading groups." A tradition at Web that remains active in several Web facilities, reading groups date to the times of Robert Fulton, a self-taught entrepreneur. Web distributes books on business and management issues to its workers, who then have opportunity to read and discuss the works on company time for forty-five to sixty minutes between shifts. The idea behind this program is to provide employees with a wider perspective and better understanding of good business practices. "We believe in learning," said Zicaro when explaining the program to President Clinton.

The American Dream

At the Chicago conference, Zicaro received special applause when he likened employee ownership to "owning a piece of the

Figure 11-1. Web Industries' commitment to people.

GROWTH THROUGH OWNERSHIP

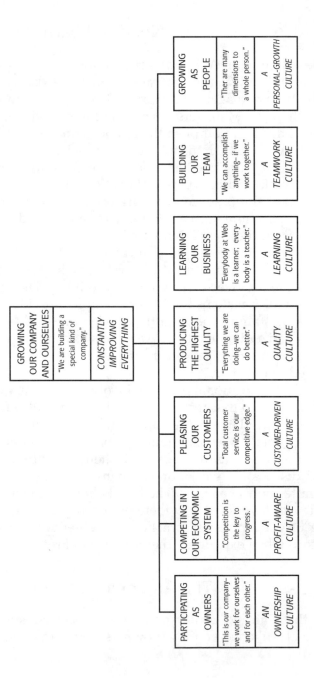

American dream." The developments at Web confirm the need for a change in management philosophy once a plan for employee ownership has been put into place. At Web Industries, this process has taken significant time and effort. Only recently has "owning a piece of the American dream" become a reality.

Conclusion

In closing, let's look back at what we learned from our review of motivation research and our visits to the eight companies, and consider where this leads us.

Initially, we learned about new research on motivation that focused on intrinsic processes—motivation that emerges from inside people. For the most part, earlier motivational approaches had been based on extrinsic determinants where people are driven by outside factors that, generally, are not under an individual's control.

Intrinsic motivation is itself the "outcome," the result of a work situation that people enjoy—because they are in charge, because they have the opportunity to acquire new skills and abilities to match a different challenge, or because they are part of a successful team. Intrinsic motivation leads to astounding creativity and productive energy that seems to have virtually no limit.

Concurrently, we looked at examples of companies with unique workplace structures and different motivational approaches. These two investigations brought us to the concepts and recommendations for "a better place to work." Three important elements must be in place to assure that people can be at the peak of their productivity:

* People need full control and autonomy at work. The job has to be their responsibility, and they must be able to

make all important decisions related to their work. At the same time, the role of management becomes one of coordinating, being available as a resource of experience and support, and serving as coaches and mentors.

* People need opportunities to learn and to master new knowledge and skills. Successful learning in itself becomes a source of motivation and builds self-esteem. In addition, learning makes people more flexible and lets them understand the interrelationships of a business (i.e., the dependence of each segment of an operation on the others). They must know enough about the enterprise to detect problems, understand the total system affecting those problems, and be able to contribute their ideas, insights, and experience to solving those problems.

* People need to be part of a work team that gives them a base of support and allows them to find their own level of challenge. Work teams make it possible to assign meaningful work segments to a group of people and broaden their responsibilities. This, in turn, makes work more enjoyable.

These three factors tend to operate as an ever-evolving system in which people develop their talents, abilities, and relationships so that the individual and the team can be more productive, enabling the organization to move on to greater successes.

Motivation, Not Manipulation

Obviously, this is a radical departure from the motivational approaches that have been practiced in the past. Our position is clearly that, as management, we cannot motivate anyone in a definitive and lasting way. We can offer incentives and rewards to get people to do what *we* want, but this will only work in the short term. We soon find ourselves looking for ever greater incentives to keep people moving, until we realize that lasting motivation cannot be accomplished by external means.

To many of us, the notion that we cannot motivate anyone long-term is disturbing. We have invested so heavily in such a great variety of motivational "machines"—from sales contests to performance appraisals, and from leadership training to analysis of personality types—that we cannot easily accept our efforts as failures.

However, we must consider the shortcomings and dangers of traditional external motivation. First, it does not last. We need to invent and design a new "mousetrap" time and again to keep our incentive systems effective and attractive enough to produce the desired results on an ongoing basis.

Second and more important, external motivation easily turns into "manipulation." Relying on the power of our position, we lean on those whom we have hired to help us, dangle money, offer a pat on the back, or voice an implied threat. And when none of this works, we may try to evaluate the worker's personality to see which of these clever stratagems (money, pats on the back, threats) appeal to his or her "way of being"—all of this just to get someone to do what we want! This is clearly not ethical and corrupts the hope of building a relationship based on honesty, respect, and mutual trust.

The implications are profound. If we accept the notion of intrinsic motivation, it implies that there is a powerful potential for self-actualization within each of us. This potential, as we have said, draws its power from our creativity, curiosity, and desire for mastery, as well as from our need for being responsible, having a positive self-image, and enjoying teamwork. Though this potential has often been stifled and crushed, it awaits ways or reasons to be released.

How can we go about implementing the concepts of *A Better Place to Work*? We stressed it earlier and would like to repeat it here: The first and most important step is to change our philosophy of management.

This means removing corporate hierarchies and top-down

power structures. It is not sufficient to simply "delegate" or "push down" authority and responsibilities if the ultimate power is maintained at the top. It means rethinking the need for executive prerogatives and perks and addressing the issue of fairness of executive compensation. It means establishing a clear code of corporate ethics.

We should open up communications and provide company-wide information on financial and other topics. Decisions should be made in the open, away from the secretive practices of the executive boardroom. This will help to establish a climate of trust and loyalty. But, most of all, we should allow people to be "human." This means showing compassion and understanding, and moving away from the corporate arrogance of justifying "tough" people decisions under the pretext of "maximizing shareholder value."

We do not have to go as far as Tom Melohn, the former CEO of North American Tool & Die, who gave himself the title of "Head Sweeper" in his book *The New Partnership*. Management is an important skill, vital to company success, and we cannot abdicate responsibility for using that skill. However, it should be a skill built on business experience, on technical or financial expertise, and on the ability to lead, to coordinate, and to build consensus. Managers need to be respected as role models, trainers, and mentors.

Once this new management philosophy is in place, it will be far easier to introduce individual and group job control, learning opportunities, and a team structure. The companies highlighted in our case studies provide insight into the ways others have handled the transition. We are sure these companies will be delighted to furnish further information.

We sincerely hope that this book helps to unleash the intrinsic motivation and productivity that appears inherent in virtually every human being. People's motivation and productivity seem to have no limit. The conclusion to our investigation—and to this Management Briefing—is that intrinsically motivated employees represent a key source of competitive advantage for our businesses. It is a reality we cannot overlook.

For additional copies of **A Better Place to Work: A New Sense of Motivation Leading to High Productivity** . . .

CALL:	**1-800-262-9699** **1-518-891-1500** (outside the U.S.)
FAX:	**1-518-891-0368**
WRITE:	**Management Briefings** **AMA Publication Services** **P.O. Box 319** **Saranac Lake, NY 12983**

Ask for **Stock #02363XSBF.** $17.95/$16.15 AMA Members. Discounts for bulk orders (5 or more copies).

OTHER MANAGEMENT BRIEFINGS OF INTEREST

Beyond Customer Satisfaction to Customer Loyalty: The Key to Greater Profitability

Identifies the four stages of a company's evolution toward building customer loyalty and summarizes the key management principles that must guide the transition. Stock #02362XSBF, $19.95/$17.95 AMA Members.

The New OSHA: A Blueprint for Effective Training & Written Programs

Explains the new law and tells which statutes are most often the subject of investigations and which require training. Models, step-by-step procedures, and additional resources are also included. Stock #02360XSBF, $24.95/$22.45 AMA Members.

Blueprints for Innovation: How Creative Processes Can Make You and Your Company More Competitive

Provides techniques, tools, and insights on how to manage creativity and innovation, based on how some of America's most successful companies support this process. Stock #02359XSBF, $14.95/$13.45 AMA Members.

The Management Compass: Steering the Corporation Using Hoshin Planning

Examines the fundamentals of *hoshin planning,* a strategic management methodology originated in Japan, that is gaining rapid acceptance with U.S. companies. Stock #02358XSBF, $19.95/$17.95 AMA Members.

Mentoring: Helping Employees Reach Their Full Potential

Shows how mentoring has progressed to an information-age model of helping people learn offering a wealth of management opportunities for organizational rejuvenation, competitive adaptation, and employee development. Stock #02357XSBF, $14.95/$13.45 AMA Members.

Quality Alone Is Not Enough

Puts quality improvement programs into perspective, and provides tools for measuring quality, linking time and quality, and achieving the shortest path to quality. Stock #02349XSBF, $12.95/$$11.65 AMA Members.

Complete the **ORDER FORM** on the following page. For faster service, **CALL** or **FAX** your order.

PERIODICALS ORDER FORM

(Discounts for bulk orders of five or more copies.)

Please send me the following:

☐ ____ copies of **A Better Place to Work,** Stock #02363XSBF, $17.95/$16.15 AMA Members.

☐ ____ copies of **Beyond Customer Satisfaction to Customer Loyalty,** Stock #02362XSBF, $19.95/$17.95 AMA Members.

☐ ____ copies of **The New OSHA,** Stock #02360XSBF, $24.95/$22.45 AMA Members.

☐ ____ copies of **How Creative Processes Can Make You and Your Company More Competitive,** Stock #02359XSBF, $14.95/$13.45 AMA Members.

☐ ____ copies of **The Management Compass: Steering the Corporation Using Hoshin Planning,** Stock #02358XSBF, $19.95/$17.95 AMA Members.

☐ ____ copies of **Mentoring: Helping Employees Reach Their Full Potential,** Stock #02357XSBF, $14.95/$13.45 AMA Members.

☐ ____ copies of **Quality Alone Is Not Enough,** Stock #02349XSBF, $12.95/$11.65 AMA Members.

Name: _____

Title: _____

Organization: _____

Street Address: _____

City, State, Zip: _____

Phone: (   ) _____

Sales tax, if applicable, and shipping & handling will be added.

☐ Charge my credit card   ☐ Bill me   ☐ AMA Member

Card #: _ _ _ _ _ _ _ _ _ _ _ _ _ _ _ _ Exp. Date _____

Signature: _____

Purchase Order #: _____

AMA'S NO-RISK GUARANTEE: If for any reason you are not satisfied, we will credit the purchase price toward another product or refund your money. **No hassles. No loopholes. Just excellent service. That is what AMA is all about.**

AMA Publication Services
P.O. Box 319
Saranac Lake, NY 12983